SpringerBriefs in Psych

Behavioral Criminology

MW00812789

Series editor

Vincent B. Van Hasselt, Fort Lauderdale, USA

More information about this series at http://www.springer.com/series/10850

Lenore E.A. Walker · James M. Pann
David L. Shapiro · Vincent B. Van Hasselt

Best Practices
for the Mentally Ill
in the Criminal Justice
System

 Springer

Lenore E.A. Walker
Center for Psychological Studies
Nova Southeastern University
Fort Lauderdale, FL
USA

David L. Shapiro
Center for Psychological Studies
Nova Southeastern University
Fort Lauderdale, FL
USA

James M. Pann
Abraham S. Fischler School of Education
  and Human Services
Nova Southeastern University
Fort Lauderdale, FL
USA

Vincent B. Van Hasselt
Center for Psychological Studies
Nova Southeastern University
Fort Lauderdale, FL
USA

ISSN 2192-8363   ISSN 2192-8371   (electronic)
SpringerBriefs in Psychology
ISSN 2194-1866   ISSN 2194-1874   (electronic)
SpringerBriefs in Behavioral Criminology
ISBN 978-3-319-21655-3   ISBN 978-3-319-21656-0   (eBook)
DOI 10.1007/978-3-319-21656-0

Library of Congress Control Number: 2015944742

Springer Cham Heidelberg New York Dordrecht London

Springer International Publishing AG Switzerland is part of Springer Science+Business Media
(www.springer.com)

Preface

The information gathered for this book began as a project for the local Broward County, Florida Sheriff, who wanted to know what the literature stated were the best practices for mentally ill persons who were arrested and held in the County Jail. At the time, he was thinking about the possibility of building a mental health facility given the expanding number of detainees with mental health problems. As we began to survey the literature, it became clear that most of the research was about programs for justice—involved people in the prisons, not the jails and detention centers, where the movement in and out is constant and unpredictable. Therefore, the information in this book is an integration of the literature we found and adapted to jails, integrating it with interviews we conducted with the jail, courtroom, and community staff and stakeholders. The questions we asked and surveys we distributed are in the Appendix. The resultant data were analyzed using a qualitative method (conventional content analysis) in order to identify themes and patterns to develop a map for best practices. This book integrates the best practice as defined in the literature, our knowledge about clinical treatment of the mentally ill, together with our interview findings from the community to develop what we believe is the current Best Practices Model (BPM). We cannot provide a blueprint for all jurisdictions here; however, we do attempt to share the integration of the literature and practice with our readers. This is presented in Chap. 1.

Most important was our finding that the best practice is to keep the mentally ill out of jail. Therefore, we also reviewed the training for police in Chap. 2 so that they are able to recognize those whose crimes are committed due to their mental illness and refer them for treatment rather than criminalize their behavior. Sometimes, it is necessary to make the arrest, but then, there are ways to defer the person to one of the specialty courts, if available. We review the most common of these "problem-solving" courts in Chap. 3; the Mental Health Court, the Drug Court, and the Domestic Violence Court. Many of those who are mentally ill have substance abuse and domestic violence issues. Consequently, availability of dual diagnosis treatment and trauma treatment is important both in the jail and in the community. Those who have been adjudicated as incompetent to proceed to trial because of mental illness or disability are usually sent for "competency restoration" and the best practices for these programs are reviewed in Chap. 4. Although the BPM suggests treatment for the mentally ill should be in the community with supervision by the courts, when they are in jail, there needs to be treatment available with seamless reintegration back to the community. This means coordination between the mental health and corrections systems. Successful programs are presented in Chap. 5.

It is clear that the challenges presented by the mentally ill involved with the judicial system suggest policies are in need of revision as indicated by a recent Department of Justice report illustrating that over 50 % of people in jails and prisons across the nation have been treated for a mental illness and/or substance abuse problem at some point prior to their being detained (James and Glaze 2006). It is estimated that at any time, approximately 20 % of all inmates will have a diagnosable mental illness that needs treatment during the time they are held in jail or prison. If the numbers of substance abusers are added to this group, the need for services would be greater than the ability to effectively provide them. This is also true if those who have suffered from trauma, especially child abuse or intimate partner violence, are also provided services to eliminate their Post Traumatic Stress (PTS) symptoms. Some suggest that our jails and prisons have, to some degree, become the mental hospitals of yesterday.

We used the local jail in our community administered by the Broward Sheriff's Office (BSO) in Broward County, Florida, as a resource in studying the issues that arise when trying to develop a BPM as this jail seemed to be similar to others reported in the literature that provide some services to the mentally ill. The number of people under the supervision of BSO at any time is estimated at 14,500 with approximately 5500 housed in its jails and 9000 placed under community control. If 50 % of this population required mental health treatment programs, the BSO psychology staff would have to serve 7250 people who have some form of a mental illness. Moreover, national studies indicate that approximately 70 % of the mentally ill in jails across the country have a co-occurring substance abuse disorder (National GAINS Center 2002). To better understand the scope of the problem, our research group reviewed some of the statistics available from BSO, Florida Department of Children and Families (DCF), and by Broward County Human Services Department regional office of the U.S. Department of Health and Human Services (HHS) as these are the major agencies responsible for the care and treatment of citizens in or out of jail in our community. In addition to adults, there are approximately 60 youth who are incarcerated in the BSO adult jail at any point in time, as they have been arrested for committing serious felonies and were waived into adult court by prosecutors. Most of these youth need intensive mental health services according to interviews conducted with attorneys who represent them, and current jail personnel and former Juvenile Detention Center staff who previously served them prior to waiver.

For the past 25 years, Broward County, like many other places in the U.S., has attempted to deal with this problem, taking a number of steps including activating several community-wide Mental Health Task Forces within the judicial and mental health systems to determine appropriate system coordination for those individuals who have both mental illness and substance abuse problems, called dual diagnosis in the literature. Most recently, the state has required all agencies to become trauma-sensitive, understanding that the service recipients often have experienced trauma and still suffer from its effects. It is important to note that these task forces have found that it is often the same mentally ill individual who needs these additional services whether they are in jail or in the community, as they often develop co-occurring disorders such as substance abuse, domestic violence, sexual assault and harassment, cognitive impairment, and the like.

Since 2000, when then President William Clinton signed into law the first Federal legislation to establish 100 mental health courts, there has been a spotlight on the plight of the mentally ill in jails as well as prisons. Broward County actually established the first misdemeanor Mental Health Court in the United States in 1997, and it has become a model for subsequent programs including a felony mental health court and mental health probation. Judge Ginger Lerner-Wren, who has conducted the misdemeanor mental health court for the past 15 years, has served on President Bush's New Freedom Commission on Mental Health (2003). Several national centers (i.e., www.gainscenter.samhsa.gov, www.consensusproject.org) have been created to assist communities in the development of programs ranging from training police to avoid arresting the mentally ill where ever possible, deferring the mentally ill who commit nonviolent crimes into community treatment programs with intensive case management, developing treatment programs for those mentally ill defendants being held in jail, and moving those people found not competent to stand trial more expeditiously into hospital or community-based restoration centers. Despite these and other strategies for better responding to the needs of the mentally ill, there are still many places where the efforts are simply insufficient to stem the flow of the mentally ill in and out of the jails, which frequently do not have adequate resources to meet their needs.

Our research group identified various stakeholders who are responsible for meeting the mental health needs of adults in most jurisdictions. This is an important first step in designing a BPM for the community. These include the local courts and attorneys representing the people, advocate groups, regional offices of state and federal agencies such as the Department of Health and Human Services (DHHS), the Department of Children and Families (DCF), and the Department of Corrections (DOC), many of whom have contracted with not-for-profit agencies to provide the services for their recipients. Other stakeholders include the Broward County Hospital Districts and various independent community health agencies and mental health providers who also deliver services to the mentally ill. Our academic center, Nova Southeastern University (NSU), is the primary training institution in Broward County for medical and mental health personnel and provides services to the mentally ill through its training clinics. As a private not-for-profit educational institution, NSU works closely with all these governmental groups. When looking at developing a BPM, it is important that there be coordination of all of these governmental entities together with other agencies and universities for the success of any project undertaken by any one or a combination of these groups.

It is estimated that the population of the mentally ill will continue to increase as a local community grows and the mental health services are unable to keep up with their needs. Furthermore, most states have faced fiscal crises with serious budget cuts in all areas of human services. Although the Affordable Care Act requires a team-based service model for health care beginning in 2014, there is no guarantee that the mentally ill will be provided with adequate services either in the community or in the criminal justice system. Therefore, it is not expected that there will be any major growth in the community in providing services to the mentally ill within the near future commensurate with service needs.

The term 'best practices' is one that has gained popularity in recent years to signify what is sometimes called 'evidence-supported practice' or simply a consensus in the literature of the most effective way to meet specified goals. The term has gained popularity in medicine and is utilized in the mental health services arena to denote practice that is supported by research and clinically based studies. A majority of BPM in any area suggest that communication and coordination among agencies is essential for a program to be successful. Dvoskin (2007) suggested that an integrated model combining intensive case management including housing needs upon release, competency restoration when needed, dual diagnosis programs (including mental health components into substance abuse treatment programs or vice versa), domestic violence intervention for batterers, and specialized treatment for women. Our findings in this study support Dvoskin's recommendations for best practices and include emphasis on a seamless continuity of care as so many of the mentally ill people regularly move in and out of jail and community.

Therefore, several elements in the BPM we propose should be in place to ensure that all mentally ill individuals are recognized and receive appropriate care, including:

1. Pre-arrest diversion by law enforcement into community treatment facilities.
2. Diversion out of the criminal justice system after arrest into treatment or problem-solving courts.
3. Problem-solving court supervision with case management and monitoring in the community.
4. Mental health treatment while in jail.
5. Competency restoration programs in hospitals and in the community.
6. Mental health probation when released from jail or prison.
7. Long-term mental health treatment in the community with seamless continuity of care.

Although this book discusses the various options for assisting the mentally ill while in the criminal justice system, in fact our study indicated that the best option for the mentally ill is to treat them in the community.

Do not criminalize the mentally ill could be our mantra.

August 2014   Lenore E.A. Walker
                                                                                James M. Pann
                                                                                David L. Shapiro
                                                                                Vincent B. Van Hasselt

Contents

Chapter 1
Best Practice Model

Introduction

This chapter describes how a forensically involved person who is mentally ill might go through a criminal justice system (CJS) that uses the proposed Best Practice Model (BPM). We understand that the costs of some of what we are recommending may exceed the current budget allocated for this population. We are also aware that the people who will utilize these services have tremendous needs in many areas besides medical and psychological, such as housing and other types of social services. Nonetheless, we have developed our BPM as the theoretical model, as if there were no constraints, understanding that all communities will have to prioritize its finite resources.

We have conceptualized this model based on the best practices literature and on the feasibility for implementation given a jurisdiction's probable current strengths. The literature and clinical wisdom all agree that the BPM should keep as many of the mentally ill out of jail and prison when possible. However, there must be a balance between public safety and best practice treatment for the mentally ill; therefore, we anticipate that some mentally ill people will end up in jail or in a locked forensic facility. Regardless, the literature suggests that the number of those who need such services should not be growing at the present rate. Consequently, there is much that the community can do to stop the flow from the community to the jail, to the community, and back to the jail, again. In the BPM we propose, it is essential for continuity of care across all the community agencies and the jail treatment facilities.

We are aware that there are many parts of this model that are currently in place in most jurisdictions. However, their full integration has not yet occurred or has the proposed system been acknowledged by all stakeholders as 'best practices.' The flow

© The Author(s) 2016
L.E.A. Walker et al., *Best Practices for the Mentally Ill in the Criminal Justice System*, SpringerBriefs in Behavioral Criminology, DOI 10.1007/978-3-319-21656-0_1

charts (Figs. 1, 2, 3, and 4) presented at the end of this chapter illustrate the way in which the system could optimally work. It is our assertion that all of the elements in the BPM need to be in place to ensure that individuals receive appropriate care including:

1. Pre-arrest diversion by law enforcement into community treatment facilities
2. Diversion out of the criminal justice system after arrest into treatment or problem-solving courts
3. Problem-solving court supervision with case management and monitoring in the community
4. Mental health treatment while in jail
5. Competency restoration programs in hospitals and in the community
6. Mental health probation when released from jail or prison
7. Long-term mental health treatment in the community with seamless continuity of care.

Misdemeanor Arrest

Figures 1, 2, and 3 depict the process that an individual with a mental illness who is accused of committing a misdemeanor crime might go through. The Crisis Intervention Team (CIT)-trained police officers (see Chap. 2) who respond to the incident need to determine if the individual is mentally ill and the type and nature of the crime (e.g., misdemeanor or felony; see Fig. 1). Police officers in neighborhoods where a relatively large number of mentally ill are known to reside should be trained in crisis intervention methods to assist in making such identifications. If the alleged crime is classified as a non-violent misdemeanor committed by an individual with mental illness, then the officer has a number of options: (1) the person can be involuntarily committed by taking him or her to a receiving facility for evaluation; (2) the individual can be referred to a treatment program; (3) the person can be taken to a crash pad, if available and time is needed to get him or her to appropriate mental health resources; or (4) the person can be arrested, booked, and taken to jail. Later, the person can be deferred into a specialty court, if available, and released from jail. It is important to note that if during any step in this process, it is determined that the individual is a significant danger to himself or herself or others, or the person cannot care for himself or herself due to mental illness, then the individual may be involuntarily committed to a facility with emergency psychiatric services. During commitment, an evaluation is conducted and used to assist a judge in determining appropriate action (usually within 72 h) or upon release from the facility. If the individual is unable to be stabilized during this brief period, then he or she may be sent for a 30-day intervention at a state hospital. If the person is still considered a danger to himself or herself or others, and adjudicated as not competent to stand trial, then further commitment may occur for competency restoration. If the person is adjudicated not restorable to competence, but still dangerous, then he or she may be involuntarily held up to 3 years for misdemeanors. If he or she is not restorable to

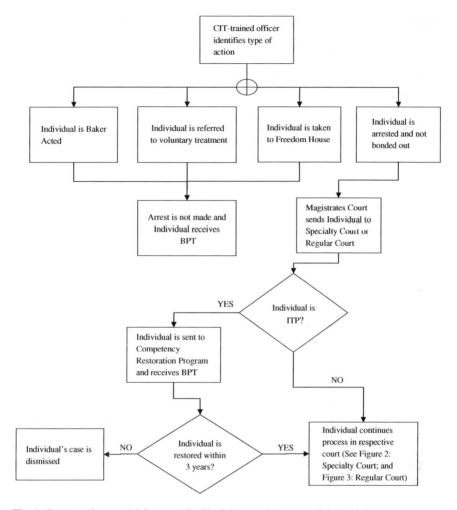

Fig. 1 Best practices model for mentally ill adult committing non-violent misdemeanor

competence, but no longer considered dangerous, then he or she may be released back into the community, according to state law. The U.S. Supreme Court case that most jurisdictions model their state laws after is *US v Dusky*.

If the individual is arrested, then his or her case is first heard at the Magistrates Court level, sometimes called, "first appearance." This occurs unless the individual is given a Notice to Appear by the booking desk or he or she is able to bond out prior to the first appearance at Magistrates Court, which is where a judge decides if there is sufficient cause to file the charges against him or her. Also at the Magistrates Court, a decision may also be made as to whether the individual should proceed to regular or a specialty court (i.e., Mental Health, Domestic Violence, Drug Court, and most recently, Veteran's Court). Participation in Misdemeanor

Mental Health Court is voluntary for those deemed eligible, and essentially, the individual has the final say in determining if he or she will go into Mental Health Court. Although some individuals who are seriously mentally ill and not receiving adequate treatment cannot competently make such a decision, the cornerstone of the misdemeanor mental health court approach is to encourage individuals to take responsibility for their own health. If the individual is arrested for a felony, then the process may be different, in which it is usually not voluntary but rather, requested by someone in the criminal justice system (CJS) as is described below.

In addition, the Magistrates Court or the regular court may decide that the individual may be incompetent to proceed (ITP), and may thus request an evaluation to make such a determination. Individuals who are determined to be ITP are sent to a competency restoration program, usually in the community, and if not restored by the time period allowed by state law, their case is dismissed. If competency is restored, the individual's case usually goes back to the specialty court. If it goes to the Mental Health Court, then the person may be diverted into a community treatment program or the case may be dismissed or adjudicated with time served.

If the person is referred to a specialty court, then there are typically three possible outcomes (see Fig. 2) in the BPM. The individual may be sent back to regular court if the specialty court is not appropriate for them (e.g., he or she decides not to participate in specialty court). Alternatively, the person may be followed closely by the judge and referred to a program that incorporates empirically supported mental health treatment. Participation in a specialty court can be advantageous as it may provide greater access

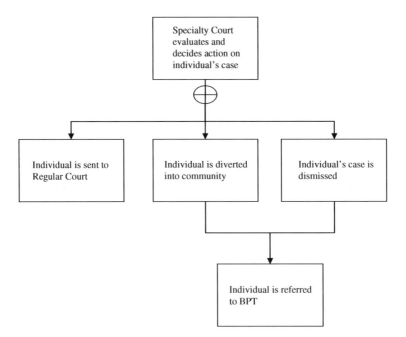

Fig. 2 Specialty court decisions on individual's misdemeanor case (continued from Fig. 1)

to community-based services that otherwise may have long wait lists, high fees, or no bed space for residential-type programs. There must be coordination between the jail facilities and the community treatment programs so that there is a seamless transition and continuity of care for those individuals. This means the program goals need to be consistent, medication (if necessary) must be continued without any contraindicated pauses or change, and space must be available in the appropriate programs. Finally, the person's case may be dismissed, although he or she should also be referred to a program that utilizes the appropriate best practice approach.

If the person is not appropriate for a specialty court, he or she is referred to the regular court (see Fig. 3). This means that he or she may be held in the jail prior to

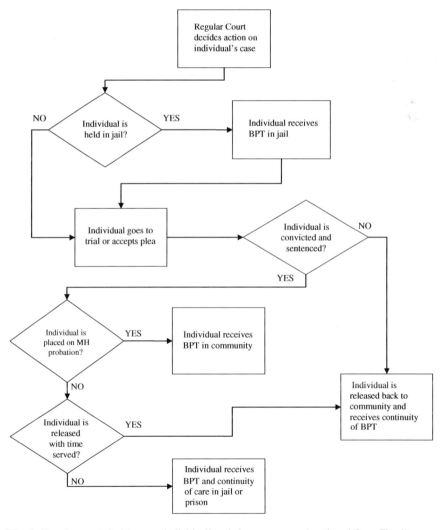

Fig. 3 Regular court decisions on individual's misdemeanor case (continued from Fig. 1)

the trial date if he or she does not have sufficient funds to make bail or bonding out is not possible due to the criminal charges or the potential flight risk of the person. Even if the person can be released on his or her own recognizance, it could take up to 21 days before he or she gets to go before another judge. Appropriate services for the seriously mentally ill waiting in the jail are necessary, and some may need to be placed on a special unit rather than in general population during the time they are detained. After a trial, the person may be convicted and serve additional time in jail, usually if the sentence is up to 1 year, although many misdemeanor cases are resolved by jail time already served. Moreover, if they are placed on probation, they should be required to receive a best practice mental health treatment approach in the community as a condition of probation. Unfortunately, in many counties, probation officers do not exist for misdemeanor convictions. Alternatively, he or she may be found not guilty and be released back into the community, but still receive best practice treatment for his or her mental health disorder. *Regardless, continuity of mental health care prior to arrest, while in custody, and after release is essential in a BPM.*

Felony Arrest

If the individual is accused of committing a non-violent felony, then the CIT-trained officer should have opportunities for pre-arrest diversion with options similar to those for a misdemeanor (see Fig. 4). It is important to note that individuals who have committed violent felonies or who have a high likelihood for violence may be inappropriate to divert into community-based programs. While in jail or a forensic hospital, some may have to be placed in a special unit.

More serious felonies, including drug charges and domestic violence charges, call for arrest and diversion into felony specialty courts. This is not voluntary as is diversion in misdemeanor cases. All those arrested for felonies should go to court for first appearance and from there be assigned to the regular court and/or a felony specialty court. In many jurisdictions, people may be seen via closed-circuit television for first appearance, so they may be in a facility other than the courtroom or the main jail. Although the jail staff screen for mental illness, if the defendant's attorney believes that the individual is incompetent to proceed to trial (ITP), then the judge may be asked to order a competency evaluation.

In the BPM, the competency evaluation should be more than a cursory screening, that is, the current practice. Although it is possible for the psychologist to determine a diagnosis after a short one to two hour evaluation, in a BPM, a standard clinical interview plus appropriate standardized psychological tests to assess cognitive, emotional, and behavioral domains should be administered and a review of the record be done to come to arrive at a more definitive diagnosis. Even then, for those who have a severe and persistent mental illness, chronic substance abuse problem, or who have been seriously traumatized from abuse, a complete psychological evaluation, together with a neuropsychological or neurological

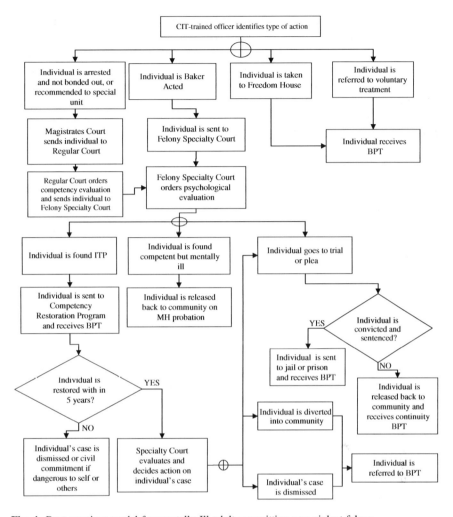

Fig. 4 Best practices model for mentally Ill adult committing non-violent felony

evaluation and necessary medical evaluations, would be considered best practice. The cost of these proper evaluations often prohibits some communities from ordering them, which may be one reason why the improperly or untreated mentally ill are in and out of jail, ending up costing the community even more money.

If the competency evaluation determines that the individual meets the state guidelines for ITP, there is a hearing and the Judge makes that finding. Then, the individual should be sent to a competency restoration program and also receive best practice mental health treatment. BPM includes medication and psychotherapy, as indicated, to assist in controlling or ameliorating the mental illness in addition to restoring competency. Simply learning the parts of the law that measure competency is not sufficient, as individuals who remain mentally ill are at the highest risk for recidivism.

In the BPM, if the individual is found to be competent but mentally ill, and has a low risk for dangerousness, then the individual may be released on mental health probation rather than be sent to the hospital for treatment. In a review of over 800 defendants arrested for a felony and deferred into the felony mental health court, it was found that over half were found unrestorable to competency no matter what treatment they received (Walker et al. 2012). Of the half whose competency was restored, most diagnosed with schizophrenia relapsed in a short period of time. If the individual accused of committing a felony does not have his or her competency restored within 5 years, then most state laws require that the person be considered not restorable and charges should be dismissed and either: (1) he or she is released into the community; or (2) if the person is deemed a danger to himself or herself or others, he or she is involuntarily committed to the state hospital until considered to no longer be a threat to himself or herself and able to care for himself or herself. As competency also refers to those who are mentally deficient with low IQ's, if the person remains mentally ill, then he or she should be referred for community treatment. This means that medication should be continuously available at the time of discharge and SSI or other disability benefits should be restored so the person can function in the community. Housing, employment, or other social services should also be met in a seamless transition process.

If the individual's competency is restored before then, he or she comes back to the court and may be diverted into a treatment program in the community, have his or her case dismissed, or go to trial in Felony Specialty Court. If the person is eligible for bail, he or she might await trial in the community or if not, then he or she is held in jail and will need mental health services during that time to be sure his or her mental state does not revert back to prior ITP status. If the person awaits trial in the community, seamless transition to the appropriate social services including housing, employment, disability benefits, and medical and psychological care needs to occur.

As might be expected, these steps take time to complete, as they require motions filed by attorneys in front of the judge. While they wait for the decisions, these defendants will need to be in mental health treatment in the jail. Special units that can provide inpatient treatment, such as is possible in the state hospital, are required for more severely mentally ill individuals in the jail to accomplish stabilization; day treatment types of facilities will be a step-down type for those who can make use of intensive all day services. In some cases, defendants may become sufficiently stable to go back into regular population provided they continue to take their psychotropic medication and attend mental health competency or treatment. All of these facilities are available at least on a limited basis in most jurisdictions.

However, for those defendants whose cases are not handled by a Felony Specialty Court, and who are mentally ill and awaiting trial, defense attorneys may feel it is not in their best interests to be in treatment while being held for trial. Therefore, the jail must be prepared to both guard their civil rights while also providing special services for these defendants. This may include special housing, medication if determined to be medically necessary, and permission to attend treatment programs, including competency restoration, on a voluntary basis.

In the BPM, Felony Mental Health Court should have the option of assigning someone to mental health probation after adjudication, whether by trial or plea, for individuals who have been deemed to be seriously mentally ill and anticipated to have difficulty in following regular probation rules. This process is beneficial as many individuals with mental illness have a challenging time strictly complying with probation rules, and the Mental Health Court judges are less punitive when individuals are non-compliant. Case management that works together with mental health probation, as well as medication and mental health treatment in a community program, should be required as a condition of the probation in the BPM.

Another way to enter the Felony Mental Health Court is through early release from the state hospital or prison. In felony cases, it is important to help the individual integrate back into the community and obtain mental health treatment immediately upon release. In some cases, these people may have been out of the community for several years and may not have had limited community ties even before they were incarcerated. Felony Mental Health Court can assist in his or reintegration into the community and work together with caseworkers to assist with employment, housing, proper medication, medical and psychological treatment, and accessing other available resources in a BPM. Mental health probation officers should be trained to work together with caseworkers and the courts so that these people have additional supervision, and get their needs met, including mental health treatment in the community.

Chapter 2
Best Practices in Law Enforcement Crisis Interventions with the Mentally Ill

Abstract This chapter describes the BPM for teaching police to recognize and avoid arresting the mentally ill and getting them the appropriate mental health services.

The first step in the Best Practices Model (BPM) is to triage between those mentally ill who continue to pose a danger to society and those who may have engaged in a criminal act that is associated with their mental illness and, therefore, would not benefit from punishment or would be deterred by legal consequences. The latter group should to be referred to a mental health provider so that their needs can be determined and services delivered in the most efficacious manner for each individual given available community resources. Diversion, then, should be to an effective community program and not into to the criminal justice system. In fact, the criminal justice system might never come into contact with these individuals if they are successfully diverted prior to arrest. A crisis intervention model, first developed by Memphis, Tennessee, Police Department, in collaboration with the University of Tennessee, is Crisis Intervention Team Training (CIT), which has become the BPM used across the country today. This model provides formal training for police officers in how to differentiate non-violent mentally ill from violent offenders, and then work in teams to help problem solving when a crisis arises. As part of CIT training, police are made aware of available resources for the mentally ill in their community and are able to direct individuals to the appropriate agency. The community agencies agree that they will have a no-refusal policy so that the interaction can occur efficiently and not take the officer away from his/her other duties longer than necessary. The goal for the individuals involved to be directed to appropriate care and not have any further contact with the criminal justice system.

Police officers have become the first responders to the seriously and chronically mentally ill. Most people diagnosed with schizophrenia or bipolar disorder, the most common diagnoses among the seriously and chronically mentally ill, are able to be stabilized if maintained on their medication and provided with intensive case management. Problems may occur when they no longer take their medication and begin to act out; however, if caught early, most can be stabilized. Even when the mentally ill person engages in a non-violent minor infraction, the benefits of getting

© The Author(s) 2016
L.E.A. Walker et al., *Best Practices for the Mentally Ill
in the Criminal Justice System*, SpringerBriefs in Behavioral Criminology,
DOI 10.1007/978-3-319-21656-0_2

them needed mental health treatment rather than arresting them are well documented. The model of community policing has been encouraging police to get to know people, including the mentally ill, in their neighborhood to resolve minor infractions and avoid making unnecessary arrests. However, police need proper training to better identify and interact with the non-dangerous mentally ill. In some communities, mental health professionals work directly with police to assist them. Many police departments also employ police psychologists to work within their department. In other communities, even those mentally ill who engage in a violent offense directly related to their illness may be deferred from jail and into community treatment.

Law enforcement is increasingly being charged with the management of severely mentally ill individuals in a crisis. Indeed, research indicates that most individuals with a serious mental illness will be arrested at least once, with many arrested more frequently (McFarland et al. 1989). For example, in an investigation of 331 hospitalized individuals with serious mental illnesses, 20 % reported being arrested by law enforcement within four months prior to their hospital admission (Borum et al. 1997). In addition to the responsibilities of management and detainment of mentally ill persons, police officers must continue to perform their primary duty of keeping the peace. These combined responsibilities present a unique challenge in their efforts to protect the public and deal with the mentally ill.

The Role of Community Policing

Over the past 30 years, law enforcement has placed greater emphasis on maintaining order and non-emergency situations, while still adhering to the primary duty of crime control (Kelling 1988; Moore 1994; Skolnick and Bayley 1986). The modern reform approach, known as community-oriented policing (COP), emphasizes partnerships, problem solving, and prevention (Bureau of Justice Assistance 1994; Mastrowski 1988). COP was based on research attempting to ascertain best practices in law enforcement. For example, Mastrowski et al. (1995) identified three COP strategies: the problem-oriented policing approach, the "broken windows" approach, and the community building approach. Problem-oriented policing encourages the utilization of resources and the involvement of civilians in crime solving activities (Goldstein 1990). The "broken windows" approach (Reiss 1985; Sykes 1986) acknowledges and adheres to the use of police attention (e.g., warnings, street stops) to minor crimes to identify problem individuals in the community. Finally, community building focuses on victim assistance (Braithwaite 1989; Crank 1994; Rosenbaum 1988) and provides instrumental services (e.g., neighborhood patrols, participation in prevention programs) to that community while deemphasizing traditional law enforcement activities.

COP involves law enforcement working closely with communities to address problems and prevent/reduce crime. This allows police officers to (1) gain a clearer understanding of activities in those areas, and (2) identify issues of concern for a

particular neighborhood or community. COP provides law enforcement the opportunity to form collaborative relationships with criminal justice and mental health
professionals, allowing for streamlined voluntary/involuntary commitments and the
identification of "breakdowns in the system" (Cordner 2000). Additionally, police
officers are encouraged to focus on problem solving in order to identify and remediate
issues or conditions that lead to critical incidents. Examples of COP include
neighborhood watch programs, storefront policing stations, foot patrols, and working
relationships with other identified community agencies (Weisel and Eck 1994).

As police officers continue to be involved in the community, they often come
into contact with individuals suffering from mental illness. In fact, police officers
have been described as "gatekeepers" to mental health services and "street-corner
psychiatrists" (Cumming et al. 1965; Sheridan and Teplin 1981; Teplin and Pruett
1992). Based on the COP approach, police officers are also more likely to be
involved not only with individuals with mental illness, but also their family
members, medical/psychiatric facilities, community outreach programs, and situations requiring crisis intervention. It is in the latter that police officers will be the
first responders; situations traditionally more suited to mental health professionals.
However, law enforcement, in general, has become increasingly aware of the need
to divert mentally ill persons to mental health facilities rather than incarceration. In
addition, many law enforcement agencies are applying COP principles to enhance
their response to the mentally ill when they are in crisis.

Models of Police Response

Law enforcement agencies applying COP principles to enhance their response to
mental health crises in community settings have followed one of three models
(Deane et al. 1998): police-based specialized police response, police-based specialized mental health response, or mental-health-based specialized mental health
response. The police-based specialized police response model involves law
enforcement officers with special mental health training who serve as the "first-line"
police response to mental health crises within the community. These officers also
act as liaisons to the mental health system. The police-based specialized mental
health response model utilizes mental health professionals who are employed by a
law enforcement agency to provide on-site and telephone consultations to police
officers in the field. The mental-health-based specialized mental health response
model consists of more traditional partnerships and cooperative agreements
between law enforcement and mobile mental health crisis teams, which exist as part
of the local community mental health service system and operate independently of
the police department.

Lamb et al. (2002) proposed a fourth category which consists of a team of
mental health professionals associated with a community mental health system,

who have made arrangements with local police departments respond in certain crisis situations when needed. While many departments in American cities with populations of 100,000 or more do not have specialized strategies to respond to mentally ill persons in crisis (Deane et al. 1998), those that do utilize one of the four specialized response models. Lamb et al. (2002) further delineate the different types of crisis response into four categories: police officers with specialized training in mental health, mental health professionals as consultants to police departments, psychiatric emergency teams of mental health professionals, and combination teams of police officers and mental health professionals.

Innovative approaches derived from each of the models are currently being implemented by police departments to more effectively deal with mentally ill individuals. An example of the police-based specialized police response is the Crisis Intervention Team (CIT). CIT utilizes police officers who have specialized mental health training and communicate directly with the local mental health system.

Program Effectiveness

According to research by Borum et al. (1998) on the three response programs for mentally ill individuals in crisis, officers from a jurisdiction with a specialized mental health team rated their program as being highly effective in meeting the needs of the mentally ill in crisis, keeping the mentally ill out of jail, minimizing time invested in mental health calls, and maintaining community safety. This investigation also found that police officers from departments rely on mobile crisis units, and on law enforcement-based social workers, both rated their programs as moderately effective on each dimension, with the exception of minimizing time invested in mental health calls (where mobile crisis units had significantly lower ratings).

Lamb et al. (2002) compared the utility of having mental health professional involvement versus training law enforcement. An advantage of a working relationship between police officers and mental health professionals is that when resolution is not possible, the number of people with mental illness who receive psychiatric referrals (as opposed to going to jail) increases as do admissions into psychiatric hospitals. Additionally, by including mental health professionals, there is potentially more information available regarding a particular individual's psychiatric history. Knowledge of prior arrest and psychiatric history can be invaluable when responding to an individual in crisis. Lamb et al. (2002) suggest that a downside to involvement of mental health professionals in crisis situations is their response time to such incidents. If response time is slow, law enforcement may not bother with requests for mental health professionals to be involved in a crisis situation.

The CIT Model

The CIT Model was developed in 1987 following an officer-involved shooting of a mentally ill African-American male in Memphis, Tennessee. The incident involved an individual with a known history of mental illness, who was observed cutting himself with a knife and verbally threatening suicide. A 911 call was made, and police officers were dispatched to the scene; the only eminent danger appeared to be to the suicidal individual himself. However, once police arrived and instructed the individual to drop his weapon (a knife), he rushed the officers, causing them to open fire and kill him out of fear for their own safety (Vickers 2000). The officers involved in this incident were White, and the individual who was shot was African-American. Thus, public perception of the event was based on already existing racial tensions of the location and time period. In fact, the outcry from the public was instrumental in the development of the original Crisis Intervention Team (CIT).

Following this incident, the Memphis Police Department, with the support of the Mayor's office, formed a partnership with the Memphis Chapter of the Alliance for the Mentally Ill (NAMI), the University of Memphis, and the University of Tennessee to develop a specialized response unit within the department. In response to a directive indicating that services were to be provided voluntarily, and at no expense to the city of Memphis, the department initiated CIT (Cordner 2006; Steadman et al. 2000).

CIT is composed of selected police officers who receive 40 h of specialized mental health training. This advanced training is usually provided by mental health experts, family advocates, and mental health consumer groups, who provide information regarding mental illness, co-occurring substance abuse disorders, and crisis intervention techniques. These officers are also informed about community-based resources for the mentally ill, receive empathy training, and participate in role plays to prepare for interactions with this population (Lamberti and Weisman 2004).

CIT officers perform their usual patrol duties; however, they are dispatched immediately to deal with crisis situations involving individuals with mental illness. Upon the officers' arrival, on-scene command is assumed. In situations where a mentally ill person is in crisis, hospitalization may be necessary. At the discretion of CIT-trained officers, subjects may be brought to the University of Tennessee Medical Center, where emergency medical and psychiatric treatments are available. Through a "no refusal" policy, stating that psychiatric facilities cannot turn away mentally ill persons, officers are able to leave the subject at the appropriate facility and return to patrol quickly. In fact, response times have been noted to be less than 10 min, with CIT officers handling 95 % of all "mental disturbance" calls, and with most officers being supportive of the program (Cordner 2006). Additionally, time spent awaiting mental health admissions is reduced, arrest rates of individuals with mental illness have decreased, referrals for treatment have increased, police injuries occurring when responding to calls involving the mentally ill have declined, and callouts for other specialized tactical response teams (i.e., SWAT) have been reduced (Borum 2000; Dupont and Cochran 2000; Reuland and Margolis 2003; Steadman et al. 2000). A recent evaluation of CIT in Louisville, Kentucky showed that CIT programs may be cost-effective and reduce psychiatric morbidity by referring seriously mentally ill individuals to appropriate treatment directly, rather than at a later point in time (Strauss et al. 2005).

In addition to the direct benefits of the CIT model, trained officers have reported benefits as well. For example, officers surveyed from each of the three previously described models rated how well prepared they were handling people with mental illness in crisis (Borum et al. 1998). Of the three sites (Birmingham, Knoxville, and Memphis), Memphis CIT officers were the least likely to feel that other officers were well prepared and were significantly less confident about the abilities of other officers than were their non-CIT counterparts. Borum et al. (1998) also found that Knoxville (mobile crisis team) officers reported that their mental health system was the least helpful. Further, Memphis CIT officers were significantly more likely to rate the mental health system as being more helpful than were the other sites or non-CIT Memphis officers. Borum et al. (1998) also noted that Memphis CIT officers were more likely to rate the emergency room as being more helpful than officers at the Birmingham (community service officers) and Knoxville sites.

Overall, it appears that officers from a jurisdiction with a police-based specialized police response capacity view their program as more efficacious in attending to the mentally ill in crisis, keeping the mentally ill out of jail, minimizing the amount of time officers spend on such calls and maintaining community safety. The Memphis CIT model appears to meet these demands and appears to be an effective program for transporting the mentally ill to appropriate treatment facilities.

Other cities, such as Houston, Portland, Seattle, and Albuquerque, have adopted the Memphis CIT model or use the Memphis model as a basis for development of CIT in their area (Lamberti and Weisman 2004). The Louisville Metro Police, with the assistance of the University of Louisville, developed one such approach based on the Memphis CIT model. Strauss et al. (2005) conducted an investigation to determine if CIT-trained officers were able to distinguish the mentally ill from other persons, and if the appropriate decision to transport the mentally ill to emergency psychiatric care was being made. Data from the investigation reflected that the trained CIT police officers adequately identified subjects in need of psychiatric services. Strauss et al. (2005) suggest that utilizing CIT programs provides an avenue for the mentally ill to receive treatment earlier, resulting in reduced costs and psychiatric morbidity.

Compton et al. (2006) investigated whether officers who received mental health training changed their attitudes toward individuals suffering from schizophrenia. These investigators found that the trained officers reported increased knowledge about schizophrenia, were more supportive of treatment programs, and experienced a change in their beliefs regarding violence and schizophrenia. These results suggest that training in CIT may reduce stigma that law enforcement officers have toward the mentally ill, result in better understanding of the mentally ill, and dispel existing myths regarding this population (Compton et al. 2006).

The CIT program in Akron, Ohio includes a 40-hour overview of mental disorders, information regarding the local mental health system, de-escalation skills, and role plays of crisis situations. Officers also train with case managers by accompanying them as they perform their duties in psychiatric emergency service centers and a consumer-directed social center. Teller et al. (2006) analyzed dispatch data following the implementation of CIT program to determine the impact of training. Results demonstrated that CIT-trained officers were more likely to transport individuals for psychiatric treatment than those officers who did not receive the training. Furthermore, results demonstrated that the trained officers were less likely to complete calls without arranging transportation of the individual in crisis. Interestingly, data from this investigation revealed that individuals with mental illness and their family members reported an increased comfort level in requesting assistance from law enforcement.

Jail diversion programs recently have been developed, in which the interaction between CIT-trained law enforcement professionals and the mentally ill is now viewed as the first phase of intervention/prevention of the mentally ill entering the criminal justice system (Lamerti and Wersman 2004). Along these lines, Munetz and Griffin (2006) developed the Sequential Intercept Model as an interface for addressing concerns about the criminalization of the mentally ill in five phases of inception: (1) law enforcement and emergency services, (2) post-arrest (initial detention and initial hearings), (3) post-initial hearings (jails, courts, forensic evaluation, forensic commitments), (4) re-entry from jails, state prisons, forensic hospitalizations, and (5) community corrections and community support. This model stresses the importance of the pre-arrest phase as the first line of interception and the point where CIT programs may impact the remaining three phases of the model.

Conclusions and Future Directions

Based on the development and subsequent investigation of CIT program models, and taking into account historical and recent trends in crisis intervention, the most effective practice for crisis intervention appears to be the implementation of the police-based specialized response program, known as the Memphis CIT model. Such programs appear to adequately prepare law enforcement officers not only for interaction with the mentally ill, but also with addressing their potential treatment needs in lieu of detaining and incarcerating this challenging population. Although there are several issues warranting further attention, (e.g., continued stigma of the mentally ill, and a lack of cooperation between police and medical/mental health facilities), utilization of the Memphis CIT model appears to be an initial step toward addressing such issues.

Despite the positive results from available research regarding CIT, there are many avenues for additional research remaining. We concur with the implications for future research outlined by Tucker et al. (2008), including advancements in assessment, the expansion of sample populations, longitudinal studies, and applications of existing research. For example, Sellers et al. (2005) found that the actual and perceived effectiveness of the Newark Police Department's strategy of treatment-focused response is equal to, and in some cases more effective than, that which has been observed in agencies with a specialized response program. Such findings suggest that specialized training may not be necessary when there are traditional, treatment-focused responses to individuals with mental illness.

Borum (2000) notes that CIT programs typically identify officers who appear to be most interested, have good interpersonal skills, and have amenable attitudes. We believe that providing comprehensive training to carefully selected CIT recruits will be beneficial by providing information regarding the differing needs of mentally ill subjects who may be in crisis at the point of contact.

There is a consensus that police departments employing a CIT model may reduce the number of situations involving unnecessary force and/or arrest. Hails and Borum (2003) found that approximately one-third of the law enforcement agencies they surveyed had some form of specialized response for dealing with the mentally ill, and the number of agencies employing a CIT program is steadily growing across the country. CIT is clearly beneficial, although continued research and training is required to foster further development of these programs. Continuing to encourage police agencies to utilize such an approach will undoubtedly improve the responses to the subjects who are mentally ill in their communities.

Chapter 3
Problem-Solving Courts

Abstract Therapeutic courts, also known as problem-solving courts, have been formed for many specific types of offenders, such as Drug Court, Domestic Violence courts, Community Courts, habitual offender courts, and Mental Health court. The commonality in all of these courts is that the focus is generally on treatment rather than punishment.

Following a new concept in judicial thinking, called *therapeutic jurisprudence*, TJ courts were developed that would help individuals solve the problems that were causing them to commit crimes that they otherwise might not become involved in. First conceived by law professors Winick (1999) and Wexler (2008), courts adopting TJ principles began to develop all over the world. The three most popular problem-solving courts are Drug Court for substance abusers, Domestic Violence Court for perpetrators of domestic/family violence, and Mental Health Court for those where mental illness was related to the illegal action they committed. Each of these three courts are conducted somewhat differently, while the defendants are deferred into either a misdemeanor or felony division and sent for treatment often in the community but supervised by the court. We discuss the three most popular of these courts in this chapter, although new TJ courts have been emerging such as Veteran's Courts and some in contested Family Court cases.

The concept of therapeutic jurisprudence (TJ), or that the law can produce a therapeutic result if the court considers the impact of a mental illness and its effect on an individual, has been shown to positively influence the mentally ill, as well as reduce recidivism (Grudzinskas et al. 2005). Therapeutic courts, also known as problem-solving courts, have been formed for many specific types of offenders, such as Drug Court, Domestic Violence courts, Community Courts, habitual offender courts, and Mental Health court. The commonality in all of these courts is that the focus is generally on treatment rather than punishment. Using the focus of treatment, these courts are able to close the gap between the court system and service providers (Casey and Rottman 2005).

© The Author(s) 2016
L.E.A. Walker et al., *Best Practices for the Mentally Ill
in the Criminal Justice System*, SpringerBriefs in Behavioral Criminology,
DOI 10.1007/978-3-319-21656-0_3

Mental Health Court and Mental Health Probation

Mental Health courts are diversion programs which believe that individuals with mental illness who commit a criminal act should be treated in the mental health system, rather than punished in the criminal justice system (Boccaccini et al. 2005). It is an integral part of "Therapeutic Jurisprudence (TJ)" or "problem-solving" courts (Winick 1999) that are now being adapted all over the world (Wexler 2008). The need for courts of this type arose from the frustration of the public and the court system with cases of the mentally ill not getting resolved quickly, the mentally ill decompensating while held in jail, and the high rates of recidivism from these individuals (Casey and Rottman 2005). Additionally, the impact of deinstitution-alization left many mentally ill individuals homeless and without treatment. Fewer available psychiatric beds meant more mentally ill individuals arrested and incarcerated for minor or even more serious acts that might have been preventable. Approximately, 25–40 % of mentally ill will come in contact with the criminal justice system at some point in their lives (Hasselbrack 2001), which leads to an overcrowding in jails and prisons (Casey and Rottman 2005; Rudell et al. 2004). Additionally, the restrictive civil commitment criteria make it difficult to mandate these individuals to treatment. In 1969, the criteria for civil commitment changed from the general criteria of mentally ill and in need of treatment with the addition of specific criteria involving dangerousness or inability to care for themselves. The new commitment laws also changed the duration of time from an indefinite amount of time to brief periods (Lamb and Weinberger 2008). The fewer and shorter commitments that resulted from this legislation meant that only the most dangerous and mentally ill people are committed. This leaves many of the individuals who may need to be involuntarily committed to get needed treatment living in the community without seeking treatment even if it were available.

The criminal justice system has pre- and post-booking diversion programs that are designed to identify mentally ill individuals who may have committed a misdemeanor or minor criminal act and divert them into treatment. Pre-booking diversion programs include Crisis Intervention Teams (CIT) of local police officers that are trained to identify the mentally ill and use de-escalation techniques to best deal with these individuals as described in the previous chapter. There are two types of post-booking diversion programs, in a court setting and in a jail setting. Both models have several benefits, including (1) the effectiveness and quality of the judicial process is enhanced, (2) mentally ill defendants receive treatment, (3) and defendants who are arrested for engaging in behavior associated with their illnesss should not be harmed by acquiring a criminal conviction (Lerner-Wren and Appel 2001). Additionally, problem-solving courts, such as Mental Health Court, have more of a discourse about ethical and legal issues (Casey and Rottman 2005). Research has suggested that involuntary mental health criteria, such as a court order, may dramatically increase compliance with medication and reduce the likelihood of psychiatric and criminal recidivism (Lurigio et al. 2004). Mental

Health court was specifically created for those individuals whose mental illness contributed to their criminal offenses and who could benefit from treatment (Hasselbrack 2001).

The mentally ill are at a greater risk for victimization, violence, and self-harm while incarcerated (Ruddell et al. 2004). The stressful environment of the correctional system often leads to a worsening of psychiatric symptoms, as well as punishment for symptoms of mental illness by the use of isolation or physical restraints (Kondo 2001; Ruddell et al. 2004). The mentally ill remain in jail approximately 15 months longer than inmates who are not mentally ill and have a less likelihood of receiving parole, due to the rule violations they tend to accrue (Bureau of Justice Statistics 2006; Hasselbrack 2001; Slate et al. 2003). The correctional system is ill equipped to deal with the influx of the mentally ill; in 2005, only one-third of the mentally ill in state prisons received treatment. For the purpose of this study, treatment was defined as psychiatric hospitalization, prescribed psychiatric medication, and mental health therapy (Bureau of Justice Statistics 2006).

Models of Mental Health Courts

While there is no set model of Mental Health Court, with each jurisdiction tailoring their diversion program to their needs, there are some commonalities. All Mental Health Courts create a special docket with a specific judge who handles only those types of cases with the primary goal of diversion into treatment (Ruddell et al. 2004). All misdemeanor Mental Health Courts require voluntary participation, which means that the mentally ill individual decides whether he or she would like to take a punitive or therapeutic course through the criminal justice system. This often causes only individuals who are motivated for treatment to choose this specialty court, which positively skews results of outcome studies of Mental Health Courts (Silberberg et al. 2001).

Also, the philosophy of all Mental Health Courts is to identify and treat individuals as early as possible. Often referrals will come from public defenders, family members, police, and other judges as soon as the individual enters the court system. Additionally, Mental Health Courts aim to reduce the stigma associated with mental illness and emphasize a therapeutic environment to reduce the trauma associated with involvement in the legal system. In order to do this, the court proceedings are often informal, with a direct dialog between the defendant and judge whenever possible (Casey and Rottman 2005). The informality is crucial in these non-adversarial court proceedings that are mental health treatment focused (Boccaccini et al. 2005). Boothroyd et al. (2003) found that, in Mental Health Court transcripts, almost half of the time (42.2 %) prior and current symptoms and diagnoses of mental illness were discussed. Also, one-quarter (24.5 %) of the cases discussed the use of psychotropic medication, and most (83.6 %) discussed treatment and placement issues.

Another important feature of all Mental Health Courts is the team approach taken. The team is generally composed of the judge, legal representatives, and treatment professionals. Additionally, case management plays an essential role in the coordination of treatment that is client centered and focuses on each individual's specific needs (Casey and Rottman 2005). This is in accordance with the terms now being required under the Affordable Care Act beginning in 2014. All Mental Health Courts consider the public's safety in their decision and have regular status hearings to review the progress of each defendant.

There are mental health criteria for eligibility into these courts. The criteria differ among Mental Health Courts. However, the majority of the courts require that an individual has an Axis I diagnosis that contributed to their legal offense. Steadman et al. (2005) studied seven misdemeanor Mental Health Courts. They found that almost one-third (30 %) of rejected referrals to the court were because the individuals did not meet mental health criteria. They also found that individuals with Bipolar, Schizophrenia, and Schizoaffective diagnoses were much more likely to be accepted.

There are also offense criteria for Mental Health Courts that differ among courts. Some courts will accept only misdemeanors, some only felonies, and some accept both misdemeanors and felonies. An example of this is the Broward County, Florida Mental Health Misdemeanor Court. This court accepts only cases that have non-violent misdemeanors, ordinance violations, and criminal traffic charges. They will not accept cases with driving under the influence or domestic violence charges, and separate specialty courts have been developed including for some individuals with domestic violence charges (Boothroyd et al. 2005). Conversely, Brooklyn Mental Health Court accepts all misdemeanor and non-violent felonies into its court (Center for Court Innovation 2006). Many courts that accept both felonies and misdemeanors will differentiate between violent and non-violent offenses, with many not accepting violent offenders (Clark 2004). The separate Felony Mental Health Court in Broward County will accept some violent offenders and does not require voluntariness for admission, taking those accused or adjudicated of a felony who are referred by others in the CJS (Walker et al. 2012). Those with developmental disabilities are also accepted into this Felony Mental Health Court.

The misdemeanor Mental Health Courts were first begun in 1997, but Federal legislation in 2000 expanded them first to 100 and then to over 300 today (America's Law Enforcement and Mental Health Project Act (P.L. 106–515). The newer models of courts tend to accept both misdemeanors and felonies, and will often include violent felonies on a case-by-case basis (Redlich et al. 2006). The Nathaniel Project, started in 2000 in New York City, is a Mental Health Court that only accepts felony cases. It will consider any defendant regardless of offense or the presence of violence. The criteria the court uses are that the individual is prison bound, has an Axis I psychiatric diagnosis, and is motivated for treatment. The Nathaniel Project will accept clients from any referral source, and then complete an intake screening to gather history. Their treatment plans usually include supervised housing or residential treatment centers due to the increase in the need for public safety with violent offenses (National GAINS Center for People with Co-Occurring

Disorders in the Justice System 2002). This is a much needed type of court because many mentally ill who do not meet competency standards have committed felonies (Fisher et al. 2006). In 2005, 49 % of incarcerated mentally ill had a violent offense (Bureau of Justice Statistics 2006). Ditton (1999) found that a higher percentage of mentally ill inmates were in prison for a violent crime, and a lower percentage of mentally ill inmates were in prison for a drug offense.

There has been a widely discussed link between mental illness and violence, especially since the mass shootings at the Aurora Mall theater in Denver and Sandy Hook Elementary School in Connecticut among others. Violence has been correlated with positive psychotic symptoms, such as delusions, hallucinations, and disorganized thinking. Violence has also been associated with poor insight, neurological impairment, and antisocial traits and personality disorder (Krakowski 2005). The majority of individuals involved in a Felony Mental Health Court have one or more of these mental health characteristics associated with violence even though their crimes may not have been with the use of violence. Furthermore, substance abuse is also correlated with violence. Substance abuse is common among patients with schizophrenia; about half of patients within the schizophrenic spectrum meet criteria for a lifetime diagnosis of substance abuse problems (Krakowski 2005). By automatically making these individuals ineligible for Mental Health Courts, the system may be failing to protect the most serious and persistent mentally ill individuals. Additionally, with no treatment, the recidivism of these felons and violent offenders is less likely to be decreased. Thus, public safety is not necessarily increased by their ineligibility, especially if they are more likely to re-offend upon release.

The success of Mental Health Courts depends on the availability of community resources, such as housing and health resources, and the ability of agency staff to monitor the defendants' progress (Ruddell et al. 2004). Service providers are often uncomfortable in the position of a social change agent, or working with a criminal population, thus refusing court-ordered clients (Watson et al. 2001). It is also common for facilities to have stringent admission criteria making it difficult to place mentally ill defendants (Lurigio et al. 2004). However, by increasing the number of defendants linked to services, the quality of these individuals' lives and the lives of those around them are enhanced. Difficulty arises in which each treatment program has its own criteria, funding, special purpose, mode, and standard of operations which makes it difficult to provide uniform treatment to court-ordered clients, and, at times, makes it difficult to find appropriate placement for an individual (Grudzinskas et al. 2005).

Many individuals involved in Mental Health Court require special services, such as competency restoration or substance abuse treatment, along with psychotherapy and close case management. It is particularly difficult to find placement for the felons who are involved in Mental Health Court because many providers do not want to accept clients with history of violence and serious criminal system involvement (National GAINS Center for People with Co-Occurring Disorders in the Justice System 2002). Even when programs are available, their effectiveness is limited by long waiting lists, lack of incentives to participate, lack of trained counselors, and the stigmatization of the mentally ill who participate (Center for Court Innovation 2001). Additionally, when these service providers fail to adequately serve their clients, the court has no real power (Haimowitz 2002). The Bazelon Center surveyed 20 Mental Health Courts, and two-thirds (63 %) of them indicated that they did not have the authority to hold the treatment providers accountable for their services (Stafford and Wygant 2005). In a study by Boothroyd et al. (2003) of Broward County's Misdemeanor Mental Health Court, it was found that defendants were referred one-third (35.3 %) of the time to an agency that had previously or recently established a treatment plan, one-third (35.3 %) referred to a specific agency that provides services appropriate for the client's assessed needs, 11 % were to initiate treatment through their own efforts, and 18 % were not explicitly stated in the transcripts based on their research. Broward County uses funding from both the Department of Corrections and the Department of Children and Families to provide these services due to collaborative arrangements.

All Mental Health Courts have regular hearings of defendants, but the period time between these hearings varies across courts. For example, Marion County Mental Health Court reviews each defendant monthly, Broward County and King County review at regular intervals or as needed, and Clark County and Santa Barbara initially see clients every week and then less frequently when they are stable (Griffin et al. 2002). However, regular follow-up appears to be a critical feature of these courts.

Sanctions are used for individuals who are non-compliant with treatment when they are involved with the criminal justice system. The types of sanctions used vary across courts from returning to court for hearings, reprimands, admonishments, stricter treatment conditions, changes in housing, and if necessary jail time (Griffin et al. 2002). Jail time as a sanction is infrequently used, but it is employed more often in newer models of Mental Health Courts that deal more with repeated felons (Redlich et al. 2006).

There are several methods of successfully closing a case, and each Mental Health Court uses a combination including suspending the sentence, adjudication withheld, no conviction entered, and a guilty plea with credit for time served. Many courts will dismiss the charges after an individual successfully completes their treatment program, such as the Clark County Mental Health Court. King County and Anchorage County all give credit for time served but the conviction may still remain on the record (Griffin et al. 2002). Boothroyd et al. (2003) found that Broward County Misdemeanor Court closed one-third (33 %) with adjudication withheld without probation, one-quarter (26 %) of cases as guilty credited with time served, 6 % adjudication withheld with probation, 5 % with guilty given a brief period of probation, and 2 % charges formally dismissed. The Brooklyn Mental Health Court, a court that accepts both felonies and misdemeanors, vacates the guilty plea for misdemeanor and first-time non-violent felony offenders if they successfully complete the court process. Other felons and first-time violent felons have their felony charge reduced to a misdemeanor, and violent offenders receive a probation sentence after successful completion (Center for Court Innovation 2007).

Individuals Referred to Mental Health Courts

There are some overall trends of the characteristics of individuals who are involved in Mental Health Courts. These individuals are disproportionately white and male, with the largest proportions in the age range of 33–40 year and 41–47 years (Fisher et al. 2006; Steadman et al. 2005). Additionally, Fisher et al. (2006) found that mentally ill individuals are arrested 16 % of the time for crimes against public order, 13.6 % of the time for serious violence against people, 10.5 % of the time for non-serious property offenses, 9.6 % of the time for serious property offenses, and 8.1 % of the time for motor vehicle offenses. They also found that a small number of untreated individuals accounted for a large percentage of re-arrests.

With the sudden increase in problem-solving courts, and specifically Mental Health Courts, there has been little outcome research done to quantitatively measure the impact these courts are having. Yet, despite no quantitative proof of the efficacy, Mental Health Courts have received governmental support.

Outcome Measures

There is significant difficulty in determining how to measure effectiveness in these courts because outcome studies typically use re-arrest as a measure; however, because of the fluctuation of these individuals' mental health symptoms and difficulty in staying on medication, relapses that might be associated with minor violations of the law should be expected (Boccaccini et al. 2005). Boothroyd et al. (2005) compared a one-year outcome of defendants who received court-mandated treatment with the outcome of defendants who did not receive court-mandated treatment. They found that those who were in court-mandated treatment had fewer arrests, fewer psychiatric hospitalizations, and less homelessness and violence. Similarly, the Nathaniel Project, a Felony Mental Health Court found success in public safety, as they decreased the arrest rates; retention, as they had 80 % retention over a two-year period; treatment, as 100 % of clients are engaged in treatment, and housing, with a significant decrease in homelessness from 92 % homeless at intake, to after 1 year, 79 % of those people had permanent housing (National GAINS Center for People with Co-Occurring Disorders in the Justice System 2002).

Henrinck et al. (2005) conducted an outcome study of Clark County Mental Health Court. They found that this Mental Health Court reduced arrests from pre-enrollment to post-enrollment. They also reported that Mental Health Court clients received more hours of case management and medication management, fewer hours of crisis services, fewer days of inpatient services, and more days of outpatient services. They also found a significant 62 % reduction in probation violations, and a 400 % decrease in the overall crime rate of the participants. Walker et al. (2012) evaluated the first four years of the Broward County Felony

Mental Health Court and found that violent crimes decreased even if the individuals were re-arrested.

Special Issues

There are many special issues discussed when exploring Mental Health Courts. A much debated topic has been the ability of these clients to understand the voluntariness of participation in Mental Health Courts. Many defendants are in a state of crisis or deemed to be incompetent while involved in this court. Thus, some people are questioning their ability to make an informed decision to participate in Mental Health Courts. Stafford and Wygant (2005) found that over three-quarters (77.5 %) of a sample of 80 defendants in a Mental Health Court were found incompetent to proceed to trial. The defendant must be able to weigh the likely sentence and period of probation associated with conviction in a regular court against the Mental Health Court program duration and its components (Stafford and Wygant 2005). It was found that in only 15.7 % of the transcripts of Broward County misdemeanor, Mental Health Court voluntariness was explicitly discussed. However, over half (53.7 %) of the clients self-reported during the enrollment process of this court that they knew that participation was voluntary (Boothroyd et al. 2003). Research suggests that individuals who feel their participation is voluntary may be more committed to treatment objectives (Kondo 2001). Further research needs to be conducted in this area and the Mental Health Courts need to take more measures to ensure the voluntariness of these individuals' participation.

Another issue that needs to be taken into consideration when exploring Mental Health Courts is the presence of co-occurring substance abuse disorders with other Axis I psychiatric disorders. It has been found that between one-quarter (25 %) and one-half (50 %) of all people with mental illness also have a substance abuse disorder, and an estimated half (42 %) of state prisoners and half (49 %) in local jails have a substance abuse problem and a mental illness (Bureau of Justice Statistics 2006). The mentally ill with substance abuse problems are more likely to be homeless, to have more severe psychiatric symptoms, to be hospitalized, to have difficulty sustaining employment, to have higher relapse rates, and to have lower rates of treatment compliance (Center for Court Innovation 2001; Watson et al. 2001). It is essential to treat both the substance abuse and the mental illness in these individuals, which often causes a problem with linking them to services. Research has shown that an integrated treatment model, or treatment of both disorders in one setting, is the most effective. Therefore, linkage to providers that deal specifically with co-occurring disorders is preferred.

While there are both positives and negatives associated with the processes of the Mental Health Court, overall, these courts reduce stigma and criminalization of the mentally ill. Additionally, Mental Health Courts link defendants to treatment services that they would be unable to acquire on their own, which increase public safety and the quality of life of the served mentally ill.

Mental Health Probation

Mental health probation is a new and emerging concept in the criminal justice system. It is based on the concept of TJ and that probation officers can serve as both an agent of positive change and a supervisor of the criminal justice system (Slate et al. 2003). Court supervised release, otherwise known as probation, typically has conditions that an individual needs to meet to successfully complete their probationary period. These conditions can include mandated treatment, a plea of guilty or conviction of the criminal charge and subsequent monitoring, no further criminal violations, required reporting to designated probation officials or agencies, no use of firearms or weapons, no out of state travel without court approval, and home visits by probation officers. This probation can be revoked for failure to comply with the set requirements or if the needs of the individual change (Silberberg et al. 2001).

It has been suggested in previous literature that 15–18 % of individuals placed on probation or parole each year in the U.S. are mentally ill; this is at least half a million individuals (Skeem and Eno-Louden 2006; Slate et al. 2004). An estimated 13 % of individuals on probation have mental health treatment as a mandatory part of their sentencing (Lamberti and Weisman 2004).

The concept of mental health probation is still in the development stages. A study by Skeem, Emke-Francis, and Eno-Louden (as cited in Skeem and Eno-Louden 2006) found that 137 of 2600 probation agencies had at least one mental health caseload, which is defined as a probation officer that exclusively works with mentally ill probationers. This only represents 5 % of agencies, although it has been reported as high as 15 % of agencies (Slate et al. 2004). Skeem, Emke-Francis, and Eno-Louden found commonalities among the existing mental health probation officers. They all had caseloads which were meaningfully reduced in size from those with regular probation caseloads. Mental health probation officers averaged 45 cases, which is approximately one-third of a typical caseload. The smaller caseload allows for more intensive supervision and linkage to services that are needed by mentally ill individuals in order to be successful on probation. They also were expected to work together with case managers. Specialists should have no more then 35 persons with severe, persistent mental illness, or co-occurring disorders (Slate et al. 2004). One-fifth of agencies with specialty caseloads officers were supervising 30 or more cases above set agency policy, which was specific to each agency. Reduced caseloads enable officers to have a greater opportunity to establish relationships with providers of mental health care and probationers (Slate et al. 2004).

Roskes and Feldman (1999) found that cases under probation or pretrial services throughout nation that involved the mentally ill had primarily psychotic illnesses. They reported that approximately one-half (44 %) of cases were diagnosed as schizophrenic and one-half (50 %) had severe mood disorders (including Bipolar and Major Depressive Disorder), and almost all of the cases (94 %) had co-occurring substance abuse. This study used a very small number of participants (n = 16), so data from this study need to be interpreted cautiously. However, a similar proportion of mental health diagnoses were found in the Broward County Felony Mental Health Court study by Walker et al. (2012). Interestingly, some defendants had up to five different diagnoses underscoring the problem of inadequate mental health examinations. Given the disproportionate numbers of people of diversity who are incarcerated in the U.S. criminal justice system, those deferred into Felony Mental Health Court were examined for similar bias; however, the numbers deferred were consistent with the numbers arrested in all of the ethnic and cultural groups (Walker et al. 2012).

Research has found that the mentally ill who are placed on regular probation are likely to have probation revoked due to new offenses (Skeem and Eno-Louden 2006), and are significantly more likely to have their probation revoked than non-mentally ill probationers (Dauphinot 1996). Dauphinot also found that the re-arrest rate on the mentally ill was double the non-mentally ill probation comparison group. She found that both groups were equally as likely to have technical violations of their probation, but that mentally ill individuals were more likely to fail to pay fines or fees and have violations categorized as other, such as failure to work. This research suggests that mentally ill individuals have more difficulty retaining work, managing their money, and being able to adequately care for themselves than non-mentally ill individuals on probation.

When developing a probation program targeted at helping the mentally ill, many factors need to be considered. Skeem et al. (2006) described qualitative interviews with probation officers, and probationers to determine the reasons why they viewed probation outcomes were influenced. The group of officers and probationers was in separate focus groups, but agreed on several factors that could negatively affect probation outcomes. These factors included officers use of negative pressures as a strategy for ensuring compliance (such as threat of incarceration); probationer–officer relationships that were uncaring, unfair, and disrespectful; and limited resources and goals of traditional probation agencies-traditional officers were not provided with resources for supervising mentally ill and not comfortable with supervising this population.

Training

In order to adequately prepare probation officers for the stress and different roles associated with working with the mentally ill population, training programs need to be implemented. Thorough training programs may also enhance the performance of these officers due to their more extensive knowledge base. Sustained officer training is common among already established mental health probation officers.

New York State probation officers training includes understanding and responding to persons with serious mental illness, co-occurring substance abuse disorders, matching services to needs for this population, developing and improving partnerships between probation and other service providers, and identification of key issues pertaining to the supervision of persons with serious mental illness (Slate et al. 2004). Federal probation officers have similar training requirements in the form of modules. Suggested components include an overview of mental health disorders, means for identifying the signs and symptoms of mental illness, the nuances of supervising persons with mental illness, and factors and rationales for special conditions of release pertaining to mental health supervision (Slate et al. 2004). Mental health probation officer training should also include crisis intervention and de-escalation techniques; an understanding of diagnoses, inpatient, and outpatient modalities; some knowledge of medications and side effects; strategies of placement and supervision; and an understanding of common behaviors of offenders with mental illness (Slate et al. 2004). Mental health probation officers should have an understanding of specific populations that could fall under their supervision, such as domestic violence, sex offender, and dual diagnosis (Slate et al. 2003). These agencies typically provide 20–40 h of training annually on mental health issues.

Mental health probation officers have a difficult and stressful role in being torn between protection of the public and providing for treatment and linkage of their probationers. While mental health officers have significantly smaller caseloads, their workload is not reduced. Specialty caseloads provide officers with time to gain better access to mental health services for their clients while maintaining a relationship with the facility to supervise the treatment of their probationer. These officers are expected to respond to minor violations with appropriate sanctions, and promote positive re-entry into society (Skeem and Eno-Louden 2006). The role of these officers is significantly impacted by the philosophy of the in agency (Slate et al. 2003). A role that is both punitive and therapeutic makes boundary-setting difficult for these officers, which additionally supports the need for training of these officers.

The community release of many of the non-violent mentally ill requires close supervision by mental health probation officers (Ditton 1999). Although Broward County experimented with four mental health probation officers, it became too costly and unwieldy to continue; instead, the probation office has trained all probation officers in working with the mentally ill.

Drug Courts

This discussion of Drug Courts has been included as part of the Best Practices Model (BPM) because of the high numbers of defendants who have both substance abuse and mental health problems. This is often referred to as dual diagnosis. Actually, Drug Courts were the first of the problem-solving courts. Although it is cost-effective and beneficial for the community to get these individuals assistance with their drug problems expeditiously, many of the more chronic substance abusers cannot stop using substances without also receiving treatment for their mental health problems, especially if they also have been trauma victims. Moreover, it is important for there to be several types of agencies in the community to receive these referrals from Drug Court. This would include agencies where detoxification (in some communities the jail serves that function) and random drug testing can occur. In addition, a residential facility is needed for those who should be out of their typical environment to begin their rehabilitation. They should deliver both trauma-informed mental health services and drug treatment for those who have both problems; and in cases where women are being treated, trauma focused services for domestic violence and child abuse. Furthermore, outpatient facilities, where integrated and separate treatment for substance abuse and mental health issues are available, and peer support groups such as AA, NA, and ALANON for families need to be available.

Reasons for Drug Courts

In the 1980s, the United States declared a "war on drugs" in an attempt to control drug trafficking and distribution of illegal drugs within the country. The government directed more effort into arresting individuals for drug-related offenses and sentencing guidelines that judges were mandated to follow, and implemented harsher sanctions in the hopes that more jail or prison time would act as a deterrent. As a result of these changes, between the years of 1980–1997, there was a 1000 % increase in the number of drug-related offenses (Wolfe et al. 2004) that were more likely to criminalize the poor and those from minority communities. Many of those most affected by these harsher sentencing laws were individuals addicted to substances rather than the drug dealers. Many of them had co-occurring disorders that included mental illness together with substance disorders. By 1997, one-third of all individuals in Federal Prison were under the influence of drugs or alcohol at the time of their offense, and 70 % of inmates had committed drug-related offenses (Tyuse and Linhorst 2005). These laws essentially criminalized substance abusers and sent individuals to prison rather than treatment facilities where they were at a greater risk of committing future crimes once released from prison.

Not only did individuals fail to receive substance abuse treatment in prison, but also they took with them the stigma of prison long after their release. As an adult, a felony conviction follows a person and impacts his or her ability to participate in the community by affecting employment, housing, and education opportunities. This stigma makes it difficult for individuals to become positive members of the community and further increases the risk for relapse and recidivism. Furthermore, research shows that increasing sentencing has little impact on recidivism, which is why the harsher drug laws have been ineffective (Spohn et al. 2001). These laws have resulted in a public health crisis in which substance abusers failed to receive treatment and caused a significant financial strain on the community.

In 1989, the first Drug Court was implemented in Miami/Dade County Florida, which aimed to divert those addicted to substances to community-based treatments rather than prison. The result of Drug Courts was to shift the focus from a legal problem to a public health concern and focus on prevention and treatment rather than punishment for certain drug-related offenses. Although not technically considered a part of the TJ movement initially, the Drug Court certainly was established as an attempt to solve the problems of those addicted to substances. Drug Courts were based on deterrence theory, working under the belief that using sanctions, defendants will recognize the impact of their behavior and recognize that there is a cost associated with non-compliance, but there are rewards for following the interventions outlined by the court (Linquest et al. 2006). This theory suggests that the more likely a person perceives that there will be a negative and immediate consequence for negative behavior, the less likely a person will be to engage in that negative behavior (Harrell and Roman 2001). This theory is the opposite of what learning theory suggests; rather, people will continue to behave in ways that bring them rewards, especially social approval. Since the first Drug Court in 1989, there are now over 275 U.S. jurisdictions with courts and 1000 Drug Courts (Wolfe et al. 2004). They have also been expanded to serve the unique needs of more vulnerable populations, such as Native Americans, women, and juveniles (Tyuse and Linhorst 2005), through treatment rather than punishment, especially as they became part of the TJ movement around the world.

Like the other TJ diversion courts, members of the Drug Court take a team approach in which the judge, attorneys, case managers, and defendant engage in a dialog to address the individual's addiction and provide treatment and community supports to decrease the rate of relapse and recidivism (Wolfer 2006). First-time offenders, who are arrested for drug-related crimes and meet the requirements of Drug Court, are offered treatment that diverts the offenders from entering the prison system. Participants are provided immediate interventions aimed at improving functioning by addressing the problems associated with drugs use, learning skills to avoid relapse, increasing family involvement, and promoting accountability for offenders (Goetz and Mitchell 2006). These interventions are highly specialized to meet the individual's needs; and, in this system, addicts are seen as patients rather than criminals. There are now special Drug Courts to meet the needs of youth who have aged out of the dependency court system, teen Drug Courts, and those to work with veterans. Like the Mental Health Courts, research suggests that Drug Courts are far less expensive than the traditional system, saving the country 1.5 million dollars per year (National Institute of Justice 2006).

Models of Drug Courts

While there is some variation between Drug Courts in different jurisdictions, they all follow a similar model. Defendants can enter Drug Court either through diversion or after they accept a plea to their charges. Today, they may also enter treatment through Mental Health Courts if they also have mental health problems. First-time offenders who have been arrested for a non-violent offense are eligible to waive a speedy trial and voluntarily enter the Drug Court program. This gets them out of jail and into treatment quickly although in some places like Broward County, there are special treatment programs for some defendants while in jail. Defendants, who have already been charged with a drug-related offense, may be eligible to participate in the court through the post-plea track if it is deemed that he or she would likely benefit from treatment. Most programs are divided into three graded steps, which are specific guidelines as to the level of treatment and court participation that is required for participants.

Individuals are expected to progress successfully through the steps of Drug Court. In step one, when a defendant enters Drug Court, he or she is placed in an appropriate treatment program as determined by the court, which usually lasts for at least six months. Generally, the court, lawyers, and treatment providers work together to decide what is the most appropriate treatment for an individual and then the treatment program to which the person is referred conducts and evaluation to determine if the person meets the criteria for the facility. When the defendant has completed this first phase of treatment, he or she may participate in a less restrictive treatment, while continuing to follow-up with probation visits and random urine analysis to assist in staying off drugs. After approximately three months, the defendant moves into the last phase of treatment, which is the least restrictive and the focus shifts from addressing the addiction to counseling, job training, and education to help connect the client with the community in a prosocial way.

Drug Courts require that participants appear in court frequently for status reviews to assess his or her progress, meetings with case workers to create appropriate treatment plans, urine analysis, and, if appropriate, to ensure the client to pay the fee for the services being provided. The court also implements various non-punitive sanctions to address non-compliance such as more intensive treatment, detox programs, new treatment programs, jail, and termination from Drug Court (Wolfe et al. 2004). The aim of these rewards and sanctions are to motivate the client to complete treatment. Upon successful completion of Drug Court treatment, the charges may be dropped or the defendant is adjudicated.

Sanctions and Monitoring

Sanctions and monitoring are key components of the Drug Court model. From a cost-benefit perspective, individuals consider the likelihood that they will be caught and punished when deciding whether to engage in negative behaviors, so if there are consistent sanctions a person is more likely to perceive a risk (Harrell and Roman 2001). In particular, many courts utilize graduated sanctions, in which as the person continues to engage in negative behaviors, the sanctions become increasingly harsher. This is different from the Mental Health Court in which the use of substances is considered voluntary even though the individual is considered an addict. This is because research indicates that individuals can learn to stop their substance use if they participate in treatment programs.

An example of graduated sanctions is the Washington court system in which the court implements harsher consequences for positive urinalysis. After the first positive urinalysis, the participant is sentenced to sitting three days in the jury box and observing court; after the second, the individual receives three days in jail; the third results in a week of detox, and the fourth offense wins a week in jail. To ensure that sanctions are implemented consistently, participants are always seen by the same judge. After the first infraction, the judge takes time to speak with the individual about the importance of complying with treatment and to ensure that the participant is aware that the judge is both involved in the case and aware of the individual's infraction.

The researchers who examined this program found that, of those who participated in the graduated sanction program, only one-fifth (19 %) were re-arrested in the following year compared to one-quarter (27 %) of the individuals who did not participate in the program. They also reported that these individuals were more likely to engage in drug treatment after they had left the court system (Harrell and Roman 2001). In general, Drug Courts tend to give judges more discretion in implementing sanctions than in traditional courts. However, it may be important to demystify the Drug Court program by implementing some standard by which sanctions are utilized.

Like in other TJ courts, judges take a broader role within Drug Courts than in traditional courts, and it is required that the judge have knowledge about addiction and the treatment resources available within the community (Wolfer 2006). Furthermore, judges are not confined by specific sentencing guidelines and can use discretion in determining who is eligible for Drug Court and how to implement various rewards and sanctions (Gainey et al. 2005). They may also use more discretion with participants taking on the role of a caregiver rather than impartial interpreter of the law. To ensure compliance among participants, judges may go beyond the rules of the court and impose individualized sanctions (Burns and Peyront 2003). Unlike traditional courts, in which the lawyer for the prosecution addresses the concerns of the state and defense attorney advocates for his/her client, the members of the court take a collaborative approach in meeting the needs of both sides rather than an adversarial one. In addition, case workers and mental health providers participate to inform the court as to how the client is progressing in treatment, and to make recommendations to the court as to appropriate referrals in the community.

Retention in Drug Court is integral to the success of the program; research suggests that defendants must be invested in the program for it to be successful (Gainey et al. 2005). It is also important to note that an individual's progression through Drug Court is often not linear; rather, it is based more on the specific person's recovery (Burns and Peyron 2003). Therefore, the screening process is an important tool used to determine who will most likely succeed in Drug Court. At this time, most courts only look at substance abuse history and the type of crime committed when determining if a defendant qualifies for the program. According to research conducted by Gray and Saum (2005), who looked at successful Drug Court participants, they found that gender, race, drug use severity, criminal history, prescribed medication, and depression were all associated with retention rates.

Research suggests that success in Drug Court is correlated with retention, and the courts utilize coercion through sanctions to enforce the rules of the program (Gray and Saum 2005). Unlike traditional or Mental Health Courts, but similar to Domestic Violence Courts, Drug Courts use more sanctions, which are treatment focused and specialized to meet the individual needs of the defendant. Sanctions can be treatment focused and include detoxification, increased time in treatment, inpatient treatment, or treatment in the jails. Judges can also sentence participants to jail time until treatment beds are available. Participants are unable to move into less restrictive phases of Drug Court until they are following the treatment guidelines as outlined by the court. For certain infractions, individuals can be removed from Drug Court and their case can then be transferred into the regular court system. Judges will use this sanction as a final option when a participant continues to be non-compliant with the program, or if the person has not been able to progress through the stages in a timely manner that would allow him/her to complete the program in the allotted time.

Time to Complete Program

Research conducted by the National Institute of Justice (2006) suggested that 12 months of treatment is the minimum time necessary for it to be effective in addressing substance abuse issues, but 80–90 % of conventional participants in drug treatment drop out before this time. Entering drug treatment through the court system ensures that participants remain in treatment for at least 2 years. Because of the structure offered, and legal pressure exerted by the courts, participants are more likely to remain in treatment compared to individuals who enter treatment on their own.

Retention in treatment is the key to success in Drug Court, as the longer a person remains in treatment, the less at risk he/she is for relapse. According to the research of Drug Court programs completed by the National Institute of Justice (2006), successful programs have a clear referral process and criteria for eligibility and incentives for participating. Participants should be fully informed at the outset of starting the Drug Court program as to the expectation of each phase. They recommend that the court balance sanctions and rewards within the program as a means of modifying behavior through positive reinforcement. This model also requires collaboration among court personnel, law enforcement officers, and human service employees.

A Model Integrated Program

Seachrest and Shicor (2001) studied the effectiveness of a Drug Court program in California in which the majority of participants were addicted to methamphetamine, a highly addictive substance from which it is difficult to abstain. The program is extremely intense and requires that participants attend treatment five days a week for six months, which resulted in few people being accepted into the program. What is unique about this program is that treatment does not focus solely on substance abuse, but incorporates acupuncture, job and GED training, and employment assistance. Furthermore, in this court model, the judge sentenced participants to state jail, which was withheld until completion of the program at which time participants' charges were either reduced or dismissed. It is possible that by being informed of the sentence, an individual facing prior to starting treatment might act as a deterrent to relapse.

Role of the Community

Unlike traditional courts that remove offending individuals from society through detention, Drug Courts provide treatment most often in community settings. As a result, it is important for the court and community to work together. Individuals who succeed in Drug Court reported more ties to the community (Miller and Shutt 2001). One of the challenges in this collaboration is that many in the community fear their own safety if drug offenders are treated in the community rather than being housed in prisons.

In one example, Harrell and Bryer (1998) examined the program Projection Connection, which aimed to connect community justice and Drug Courts. According to this model, community justice was defined as individuals and communities that were affected most by drug-related crimes. The goals of the program were to collaborate with community members, reintegrate offenders into the community, engage offenders' families in treatment, and address quality of life concerns. Criteria for offenders to qualify for this program were a previous substance abuse diagnosis and a history of non-violent offenses. The program sought to engage community members in the judicial system by showing them how Drug Courts and community re-integration could decrease recidivism and increase safety within their neighborhoods. To do this, the program developers engaged in community outreach to inform individuals about the projects, learn about community resources, and get feedback so that people in the community felt engaged and empowered. To further support collaboration, the court published a newsletter and utilized open houses to educate the community about how the courts worked.

The program also went into the schools to educate students about drugs and the court system. Rather than using the traditional Drug Courts, which serve large areas, they implemented Community Courts, which served specific geographic areas and addressed victimization of community members. Community members were also invited to volunteer in the courts. The offender had the opportunity to communicate with community members in town hall style meetings in which they could discuss the impact of addiction and link the offender to a community organization to ease re-integration. The families of offenders were included in treatment through education about substance abuse and community resources, as well as involving them in the recovery process.

Finally, the police participated by monitoring offenders in the community, expediting warrants issued by the treatment courts, attending graduation ceremonies for participants, and engaging in training programs to increase their awareness about addiction (Harrell and Bryer 1998). A program, such as this, seeks to bridge the gap between the judicial system and the communities most impacted by substance abuse and crime. Many Drug Court programs fail to address the needs of these communities and the challenges of re-integration once an offender completes drug treatment. It is important that issues of re-integration be addressed to decrease the risk of recidivism. This includes retraining and employment needs, issues that arise with children (especially for women), and connections within the larger community.

Collaboration with Mental Health Professionals

In order for Drug Courts like Mental Health and other TJ courts to be successful, there must be appropriate treatment facilities within the community for referrals. According to Tyuse and Linhorst (2005), there is limited access to treatment facilities when there are too few treatment programs available for the court to refer clients. It has been suggested that there is a need for increased collaboration between mental health professionals and the court to improve screening to weed out individuals who may be less likely to succeed in treatment programs so as to use the treatment space most effectively (Gray and Saum 2005).

In 2007, California initiated Proposition 36, a Drug Court program, so that drug-addicted offenders would receive treatment rather than punishment in an aim to decrease recidivism. An unintended side effect of this program was the decrease in availability of treatment for non-Proposition 36 clients. Each year since the implementation of Proposition 36, there have been 8000 fewer individuals seeking voluntary substance abuse treatment. In the second year, one-third of the treatment providers reported that there were fewer treatment beds available for individuals seeking treatment on their own rather than being referred by the courts. Furthermore, they reported that individuals who entered treatment through court referrals differed from self-admit clients. Based on these data, there is a need for more treatment facilities to house the growing number of referrals made by the courts (Hser et al. 2007).

Limitations of Drug Courts

In many ways, Drug Courts challenge the basic premise of the legal system providing what is called 'Due Process" and "proportionality' (Berman 2004). By giving judges more freedom to issue individualized sanctions, rather than following general guidelines, there is a danger that treatment may be provided at the sake of fairness to other defendants charged with the same crimes, and there is a greater risk for discrimination to occur.

Discrimination

According to research conducted by Lowenkamp et al. (2005), offenders who commit more serious crimes tend to receive harsher sanctions, and non-white offenders are given alternative sanctions more often than probation. Based on this research, when there is limited information, judges may rely on stereotypes when making decisions about sanctions and probation. For example, Gaincy et al. (2005) found evidence of inequality in the way alternative sanctions were implemented based on gender and race. Researchers have also theorized that staff are more likely to negatively interpret the behavior of minorities, including that they are more likely to come from a low socioeconomic background and that there will be less family involvement in treatment (Seachrest and Shicor 2001). In particular, they found that overall, males were less likely than females to receive alternative sanctions. They also noted that racial minorities, especially Hispanic males, received alternative sanctions less often. Furthermore, the researchers found that there was variability in the way in which sanctions were implemented between counties.

As part of their research, the evaluators relied on qualitative data from people working in Drug Courts. While respondents denied that ethnicity played any part in sentencing, the Public Defenders who were interviewed suggested that the judges were more sympathetic to defendants who looked like them. There can also be inconsistency in how judges rotate through the court resulting in varied implementation of sanctions and rewards based on judge's discretion (Wolfe et al. 2004). Drug Court programs have been criticized for not having treatment programs that are tailored to meet the unique needs of females and minorities (Bouffard and Taxman 2004; Walker 2009). Due to the ambiguity in Drug Courts as to how treatment and sanctions are used, offenders may opt out of Drug Court if given the opportunity. Critics also argue that because Drug Courts do not follow the adversarial model of traditional courts, the attorneys fail to represent clients effectively (Berman 2004). Of course, these problems can occur in any of the traditional and other problem-solving courts. It highlights some of the issues when a correctional and mental health system attempt to work together. Research on the Felony Mental Health Court examined racial and ethnic disparities and found that they were consistent with traditional arrests (Walker et al. 2012).

Theoretical Issues

There has been some conflict between typical mental health approaches, such as Cognitive Behavioral Therapy (CBT), which teaches control over thoughts and behaviors, and the principles of the NA/AA model which suggest that substance abusers must turn to a higher power and surrender control. However, despite the theoretical differences, CBT remains the only intervention model that has data supporting its efficacy. Using a more eclectic model, it was found that treatment providers failed to spend enough time on any one intervention or issue. Furthermore, many substance abuse programs could not provide ancillary services that were an important component of relapse prevention such as education, and mental and physical health. None of the groups that were observed by Bouffard and Taxman (2004) incorporated the families in treatment. Some substance abuse programs are actually unwilling to incorporate mental health services into their program, and often they do not have any adequately trained mental health practitioners on staff.

Throughout the research, there is evidence that minorities tend to be less successful in completing Drug Court programs as compared with Caucasians, and there appear to be a number of factors to account for this difference. One important component appears to be based on perception of the courts and treatment. There are a disproportionate number of African Americans participating in Drug Court as compared with other groups; however, much of the research has suggested some inequality in the way minorities who do participate are treated within Drug Court. According to research conducted by Cresswell and Deschenes (2001) in California, African Americans reported distrust in substance abuse treatment. Minorities were more distrustful of treatment than prison and were more likely to opt out of Drug Court. Perhaps, this distrust is due in part to the ambiguity associated with Drug Court as compared with traditional sentencing. Due in part to the racial inequality that continues to prevail in mainstream society, minorities may fear that the courts and treatment facilities will treat them unfairly. Research suggests that minorities view sanctions in Drug Court as more harsh than prison (Cresswell and Deschenes 2001). Perhaps, Drug Courts may benefit from implementing graduated sanctions as was done in the Washington, DC court, which implemented specific consequences for infractions (Harrell and Roman 2001), or consider the Mental Health Court model where there are minimal sanctions.

Individuals in Drug Court receive sanctions when they fail to comply with the requirements of the program. However, as Wolf and Colyer (2001) found, many of the factors associated with non-compliance are beyond the control of Drug Court participants. In their study, they assessed the types of problems identified by clients in a New York State Drug Court to find ways to improve treatment success. They found that the most commonly identified problems were treatment availability, difficulty with their primary support group, health issues, problems associated with the justice system, and unemployment. They categorized the problems into three groups: those that fell under the control of the individual (immediate), his/her specific environment (intermediate), and problems associated the social environment (structural). The researchers found that all of the participants being assessed identified some problems associated with the social environment; and because these are related to the larger social system, individuals were less able to manage these problems (Wolf and Colyer 2001).

These findings suggest that evaluators should assess these problem areas when a client begins treatment so as to determine the specific needs of the individual. Efforts can then be made to link him/her with necessary supports to prevent these problems from interfering with the individual's ability to succeed in Drug Court. It is possible that clients may be sanctioned and considered non-compliant in Drug Court at times when they are experiencing problems that are beyond their individual control. For example, clients who are struggling financially trying to support a family and maintain steady employment may find it challenging to meet the strict attendance requirements of treatment programs.

There is little information in the literature on the role of psychologists in assessing readiness for change and appropriateness for Drug Court. Many individuals with substance abuse issues also qualify for a psychiatric diagnosis. Most states have multiple special courts including Drug, Mental Health, and Domestic Violence Courts, and since problems are often co-occurring, it may difficult to determine in which court an offender should be placed. This is of particular importance because the type of alternative court in which an offender is placed will direct the focus on treatment. Consequently, if a person qualifies for a dual diagnosis, it is important to assess how the diagnoses interact and in what type of treatment facility the person would be most successful. Psychologists are frequently used in Mental Health Courts to complete competency evaluations and make treatment recommendations for participants. Such evaluations may be useful in Drug Courts as well to determine which court is most appropriate for the individual.

According to research conducted by Miller and Shutt (2001), in some counties, as many as 90 % of Drug Court participants drop out of the program prior to graduation. In particular, they examined the Drug Courts in Richland County, South Carolina in which there is an 89 % drop out rate. In this county, only 39 % of individuals who are eligible for Drug Court are admitted due to limited resources within the court and community. These statistics further stress the importance of conducting thorough assessments to determine eligibility for the program. They identified certain factors associated with failure, including addiction to crack, prior criminal history, younger age of onset, and a history of personal offenses. The researchers suggested that by identifying these factors they could predict failure (Miller and Shutt 2001). This information is certainly useful in identifying individuals who may struggle in treatment. However, by potentially barring these individuals from the program, Drug Courts are essentially turning away the individuals most in need of treatment. Researchers have also suggested that, due to their perception of them, judges are harsher toward crack addicts, which may be why they are more likely to fail in Drug Court (Saum et al. 2001).

On the other hand, much of the research suggests that Drug Court graduation is a key component in preventing relapse and recidivism. By assessing these factors, courts could ensure that treatment goes to those who are more likely of successfully completing the program. Furthermore, Miller and Shutt (2001) suggest that admitting individuals into Drug Court who are likely to fail will result in their spending more time in prison than if they were to opt into traditional court because of sanctions.

Drug Court and Violent Criminals

In almost all Drug Court programs, individuals are deemed ineligible if they have been arrested for violent crimes. The problem is that with overcrowding in the jails many violent criminals with substance abuse issues are placed under community supervision, and without treatment they are at greater risk for recidivism (Saum et al. 2001). Violent criminals pose a more significant threat to our communities. Spohn et al. (2001) found that violent criminals who used heroin were 15 times more likely to commit robberies, 20 times more likely to commit burglaries, and 10 times greater risk of engaging in thefts than non-drug users. Furthermore, in some states, individuals are charged with a violent crime when they are arrested for drug possession if the quantity of drugs is significant. The researchers reported that older criminals were more likely to succeed in Drug Court and abstain from engaging in future criminal behavior even though they were more likely to have a longer and more violent criminal history compared to youths who may have been arrested for their first crime. They found that individuals with longer criminal histories fared worse in treatment than those with violent criminal histories (Saum et al. 2001).

Restitution

In Broward County, Florida, many clients are required to pay restitution as part of Drug Court. Those who are experiencing financial hardships and unable to pay these fees cannot progress to less restrictive phases of the program even if they are compliant with treatment and abstaining from substance abuse. The problem with this requirement is that, in the less restrictive phase of treatment, a person is able to focus more on finding employment, which would make it more likely that he or she could pay restitution. As Wolf and Colyer (2001) suggest, it is important for the court to take into account the unique issues with which participants may struggle that impact their success in treatment.

Research evaluating Drug Courts compared with traditional courts suggest that the former are associated with increased involvement in treatment and decreased recidivism. However, much of the research to date involves small sample sizes and because of this, it may difficult to generalize findings (Tyuse and Linhorst 2005). As the number of Drug Courts across the country continues to grow, more extensive evaluations should be conducted using larger samples to determine the effectiveness of Drug Courts compared with traditional courts.

Conclusions

Drug Courts offer an alternative way of conceptualizing and addressing many individuals who are arrested for drug-related offenses in which they are seen as victims of addiction rather than criminals. As a result, they are offered treatment as opposed to incarceration. The aim is to address the underlying addiction that leads to criminal behaviors so as to decrease the risk of recidivism. Much of the research on Drug Court programs across the country suggests that they are effective in addressing substance abuse and decreasing the risk of future involvement in the criminal justice system. In particular, individuals who successfully graduate from these programs appear to be better able to manage their addiction and avoid future involvement in the legal system.

One of the shortcomings of Drug Courts is the limited resources available in terms of psychotherapy and drug treatment facilities in the community, trained court personnel, and ancillary services which improve the likelihood of success. This is true in Broward County as well. There are different Drug Courts that follow the State Statutes requiring 2 years of treatment. However, there does not appear to be communication between mental health and substance abuse treatment providers for those with co-occurring disorders. Increased funding should be provided to increase the availability of resources. In addition, court and treatment staff should work together to develop more comprehensive screening measures to assess individuals' ability to succeed in such a rigorous program. These assessments should (1) address the specific needs of the individual, (2) identify potential problem areas, (3) remove barriers to accessing treatment, and (4) evaluate and increase individual's motivation to change.

Domestic Violence Courts

Domestic Violence Courts are another type of problem-solving court. We included a review of best practices for Domestic Violence Courts because of the high overlap with mental health issues, especially for the victims. Those who are arrested for spouse abuse are usually men who may have engaged in domestic violence many times before the first arrest. The goal for this court is twofold; first, to provide safety to the victim; and second, to assist the perpetrator in stopping the abusive behavior. When the Domestic Violence Court was first designed, it was important to help the criminal justice system understand that family violence was a criminal act. The Department of Justice (DOJ) held hearings for victims of crimes around the country in 1982 and excluded testimony from victims of domestic violence. Battered women advocates protested this exclusion and in 1983, the DOJ held hearings with domestic violence victims who demanded prosecution of the batterer together with the opportunity to be referred to specific domestic violence treatment. The early Domestic Violence Courts provided protection for the victims by assigning them advocates from the prosecutors' offices, usually called victim-witness advocates, and taught victims how to apply for restraining orders without having to file for divorce or other civil matters.

A best practices approach is one where these services are available for victims and includes holding the alleged perpetrator at least 24 h overnight in jail and then offering referral into a treatment program if the victim is safe. Domestic Violence Court judges who issued temporary orders of protection also were able to award temporary custody, child support, and maintenance and exclusive use of the home. Restraining order hearings to make them permanent and give the alleged perpetrator the opportunity to rebut the order could elect to do so in front of a judge who was trained to understand the dynamics of domestic violence and the possibilities of recantation by frightened victims. Treatment programs approved by the court should offer offender-specific treatment with providers having regular contact with the victim and the court, so that offender infractions are dealt with immediately. Offenders who are court-ordered, or who volunteer to enter these programs, should be monitored for attendance and behavior change. Unfortunately, over the years, treatment programs have varied in terms of the type of intervention offered to perpetrators, and the ability to follow-up with immediate consequences for not following the intervention has been sporadic. The current research literature suggests that not all domestic violence intervention programs are successful in stopping the violence.

The philosophy around domestic violence has evolved in the past 40 years with most people agreeing that violence in the home is no longer a private matter, but a serious crime plaguing all societies. The U.S. Attorney General's Task Force on Violence in the Family in 1983 recommended criminalizing domestic violence, the United Nations soon followed, and most countries have adopted similar laws. This change in thinking has had implications for many disciplines including, but not limited to, the police and the legal system. Many states have recognized that the crimes considered domestic need to be handled differently than non-domestic crimes in the court system. One important reason is that, unlike non-domestic crimes, these crimes are charged with emotion as they involve people who have relationships; and in many cases, the relationships will not necessarily end with the adjudication of the case. Another reason is the co-occurrence of domestic violence with mental illness, substance abuse, and trauma triggers from earlier child abuse. Consequently, part of the family court role is to be thoughtful about and monitor the continuing relationship between the parties, while community agencies and the jail need to be aware of the interactions between all three problem-solving courts. Recent research into murder-suicide rates suggests that child custody disputes in family court, usually by those with domestic violence allegations and histories put people at high risk for such incidences (Lopez et al. 2014).

As a result, many prosecutors' offices have introduced victim-witness advocates who work closely with domestic violence victims to successfully prosecute the batterer and give him the opportunity to attend specific treatment programs for offenders. In many of these jurisdictions, the court is able to refer to batterer treatment programs that are approved by the local or state authorities. Recommendations for domestic violence courts include vertical prosecutions, support for victims and referral to community battered women shelters and task forces, special treatment programs for offenders, no contact orders where appropriate, and temporary exclusive use of the home and custody of children to be issued by the domestic court judge with later coordination with child dependency and family courts, if applicable.

According to U.S. Department of Justice (2005), about one-quarter (22 %) of murders in the year 2002 were perpetrated by family members, with nearly 9 % murders of a spouse, 6 % were murders of sons or daughters by a parent, and 7 % were murders by other family members. Although these statistics reflect only fatalities, family violence crimes recorded by the police in the District of Columbia and 18 states comprised one-third (33 %) of all violent crimes with more than half of them between partners (U.S. Department of Justice 2005). This percentage is staggering, in which many police departments report roughly one-third of calls for service as domestic in nature. In addition, police receive a high percentage of repeat calls for service involving the same offenders and victims. Similarly, in New Haven, Connecticut, domestic violence accounts for approximately 30 % of police calls for service and of these, 29 % require repeat police calls over time, and are considered most dangerous for officers, victims, and children (Shaffer and Gill 2003). A recent study of homicide-suicides in Florida found that the largest numbers of homicide-suicides involved domestic violence, adding to the complexity of the problem (Lopez et al. 2012).

Police calls for service of domestic issues comprise such large percentage of police activity and are often considered the second most dangerous type of call for police officers to respond. They are also often reported by police to be the most frustrating and time consuming. These elements may impede the attention to detail and delivery of services by police to the victims that need the services the most: battered women and children (Casey et al. 2007).

The literature is abundant in noting the negative effects on children of exposure to violence in the home. Marans (1998) notes that children who are chronically exposed to violence develop symptomatology that impairs their emotional, psychological, educational, and cognitive development. Also noteworthy is that in poor urban areas where the prevalence of all types of violence is high, "there may be a natural progression from witnessing (violence) to being the victim of (violence) and then to engaging in violence" (Marans 1996). The large-scale study of Adverse Childhood Events (ACE) conducted by the Centers for Disease Control (Felitti 2001) found exposure to violence in the home one of the largest contributors to major health problems later in life.

Models of Domestic Violence Courts

Individual jurisdictions have developed court models that begin with the same premise: Domestic cases need to be handled by a court dedicated to these complex issues. However, each state implements court protocols differently according to resources and philosophy. In addition, states vary in their definitions of what falls under the umbrella of a domestic violence offense. For example, in Connecticut, a special docket has been created with the sole purpose of hearing, monitoring, and adjudicating cases that fall under this umbrella. One judge is assigned to the docket so that the same judge sees perpetrators who violate court orders. This concept is one of a vertical prosecution in the hope that having to be in front of the same judge will become a deterrent to re-offend. In addition, this court works closely with the agency that provides social services to the victims of domestic violence. It works so closely, in fact, that victim advocates are housed in the courthouse to allow for immediate intervention and referrals at the time of arraignment (Gill 2006).

One program analysis by Gondolph (1999) hypothesized that the re-arrest rate would decrease when offenders completed a comprehensive program with extra services available to them. Four groups were analyzed: a pretrial group for three-month duration with additional service referrals; a three-month post-conviction group including referrals and assessments as well as a women's and a children's group; a six-month post-conviction group with referrals and assessments with women's groups; and a nine-month post-conviction group that included evaluation and in-house treatment for substance abuse, and mental health issues and women's casework.

Results found differences in re-assault rates only in the nine-month duration group. A significant difference was noted in severe and repeated assaults between the two: three-month program and the nine-month program. As hypothesized, women with partners in the nine-month program reported feeling that they would not be hit again, but there were no differences between the groups as feeling safer. Contrary to the hypothesis, women in the shorter duration programs reported feeling better off than those in the longer program. This makes sense, as the re-assault rates for the men who attended three months of sessions were significantly lower than the nine-month group men. This difference could be attributed to the fact that the court reviewed the case at three months, thus serving as a deterrent to re-offend. It may be that close court monitoring and accountability can serve to decrease future violence.

Another hypothesis regarding re-offense has to do with the motivation of the individual. Dalton (2001) employed a longitudinal study design to examine whether or not men who perceived more external pressure would be more likely to complete a batterer treatment program. This hypothesis stems from the suggestion in the literature that batterers are not intrinsically motivated to change their violent behavior, but will do so when external pressures are in place. Interviews were conducted upon entrance to one of two programs, followed by chart reviews to discern treatment progress five months after the interview.

The hypothesis in this study was not supported, as the level of perceived external pressure did not predict program completion. This study has a possible confound, in which the men who participated were those men who actually came to treatment, not the ones who were referred but did not comply. Another possible confound is the program rule that nonpayment of treatment resulted in dismissal from the program. Also, it is important to note that neither program addressed other issues, such as substance abuse and unemployment, which could affect program attendance.

Feder and Dugan (2004) examined whether lower rates of violence would be found when men convicted of misdemeanor domestic violence offenses were mandated by a judge to attend either an experimental group or a control group. The experimental group consisted of one-year probation and attendance at one of five local Spouse Abuse Abatement Programs (SAAP), all based on the Duluth model of intervention. The control group consisted of men who only received one-year probation. The hypothesis was that these men with a high stake in conformity, operationally defined as employment, marital status, age, and residential stability, would exhibit lower rates of repeat violence. All men were interviewed at adjudication and six months later; victims were interviewed at adjudication as well as six and 12 months later. The groups were found to be similar in demographics, stake in conformity, and criminal record. However, the control group had a mean age two years younger than the experimental group. Also similar were mens' belief in responsibility for wife beating and attitudes regarding women's roles.

At the six-month mark, no differences were found between both groups for use of violence with 30 % self-reporting using minor violence, and 8 % admitting to using severe violence. Interestingly, younger men without stable residence were significantly more likely to report violent incidents. Again, with respect to stake in conformity, age and employment were significantly related to re-arrest, while marital status and residential stability were not. The number of months employed was significantly and inversely related to the likelihood of re-arrest.

Almost one-quarter (24 %) of men in both conditions were re-arrested within the year. However, the men who attended all classes were significantly less likely to be re-arrested, while men who attended fewer classes were 2.5 times more likely than the control group to be arrested. This study concluded that the men who do not seem to be deterred from missing their court-mandated treatment are also not deterred from the consequences of re-arrest.

Dobash and Dobash (2000) compared two court-mandated programs for men guilty and on probation for domestic violence with a group of similar men receiving traditional treatment such as fines, probation, and prison time. Information was also gathered from the female victims. The participants had similar criminal histories, but the men in the program group were more likely to be employed. Evaluations were completed at three intervals: intervention time, three months, and again at 12 months, Time 1, 2, and 3, respectively. The program group included participation in group work with a psychoeducational approach in which the men were provided with education about violence as a learned behavior and the need to take responsibility for their use of violence.

The group portion of the intervention was intensive, in which eight stages of a "transformative process" were covered. They are as follows: recognition that change is possible, gaining motivation to change, consideration of costs and benefits of change, viewing the self as a subject and not an object, shifting change internally as opposed to external constraints, using words and ideas that reflect nonviolence, adopting new ways of thinking that require talking and listening to others, and learning new ways and skills for conflict resolution. This comprehensive intervention enabled men to take responsibility for their use of violence and to appreciate the fact that they made a choice to use violence.

The programs seemed to reduce mens' use of violence as well as eliminate violence after several months to a year. The men were also less likely to use intimidating and controlling behaviors. Women with partners in the program groups reported significantly more than the women with partners in the comparison group that their quality of life was better as measured by them feeling safer, a better sense of well-being, and positive improvements in their relationships. Quality of life changes for both men and women was more likely to be seen in men who completed the program.

However, 7 % of the men in the program were re-arrested at follow-up as compared to 10 % of men receiving traditional sanctions. By women's report, the men in the program group used violence significantly less in the two time periods (30 and 33 %) as compared to the criminal justice group (61 and 69 %). Given this difference, it was also noted that the 25 % of the comparison group remained violence free. Also noteworthy was that at Time 1, there were slight differences between the groups and violence usage compared to Times 2 and 3 where it was significant (Dobash and Dobash 2000).

The efficacy of batterer's treatment programs has not yet been empirically proven despite the fact that most women advocate groups believe that battered women are more likely to take steps to protect themselves, such as making police reports, when there is a batterer's treatment program available (e.g., Battered Woman's Justice Project; Hart and Klein 2013). However, others, such as the Honorable Marjory Fields, the retired Chief Judge of the New York Supreme Court, Bronx Family Court states that her experience was that diversion into batterer treatment programs usually was less effective in stopping the violence as compared to swift punitive responses from the judicial system (Fields 2010).

Safety for Children in Domestic Violence Homes

Shepard and Rashchick (1999) found, by interviewing child welfare workers, that although over one-third of the cases referred to this child protection agency had known domestic violence issues, no formal or systematic protocol was in place. Furthermore, domestic violence was rarely mentioned in court proceedings even though 14 out of 19 cases were identified as being at significant risk. The other five cases were only mentioned as relevant to protective order hearings.

Workers directly assessed domestic violence in 45 % of the referred cases, but this was by asking at least one of three assessment questions. In 35 % of the cases, the worker asked all three questions. Although most workers did ask about domestic violence, the focus was only on the victim's immediate safety needs without further probing or even providing them with additional support and information. Workers often (92 %) utilized at least one domestic violence intervention. However, this only included safety issues, information on crime and calling police, and the dynamics of domestic violence. Specialized referrals—such as shelters, women's groups, written material, restraining, and protective orders—services for children, and an active involvement—such as arranging to check-in by phone with the client—were very rarely employed. Given the overlap of partner abuse and child abuse, child protection agencies need to have a more collaborative relationship with the other disciplines involved in domestic violence.

The area where the least amount of protection for children has been noted in the family courts is when the parents are separating or divorcing (Walker et al. 2012). Here, it has been noted that the presumption that access to both parents is in the child's best interests has placed both the children and their mothers in danger from all forms of abuse (Chesler 2013). Kleinman and Walker (2014) have criticized the Association of Family and Conciliation Courts (AFCC) published guidelines for those involved in court-ordered therapy as adding to the lack of protection of women and children. Saunders et al. (2011) interviewed custody evaluators and judges and found bias against mothers when abuse was reported in family court proceedings. Many Fathers' Rights groups have been used by batterers to demand custody of their children, to avoid paying child support, or as revenge against their mothers for terminating the relationship (Bancroft and Silverman 2002; Walker 2009). Mothers who have lost custody of their children, often through the court's believing allegations of a non-existent 'parental alienation syndrome' or other biases, have begun forming alliances and petitioning legislators to change the laws to better protect children (e.g., The National Coalition for Family Justice (www. ncfj.org). Children have formed organizations to support each other and try to prevent others from being removed from their mother's custody (e.g., www. courageouskids.net).

Women Arrested for Domestic Violence

Miller (2001) conducted information-gathering interviews with members of several disciplines including criminal justice professionals, social service providers, directors and case workers of battered women's shelters, victim service workers affiliated with the police department, probation officers, prosecutors, social workers, providers of arrested women's groups, and family court advocates. These inter-views were designed to provide insight on the issues that arise from arrests of women for domestic violence.

Results showed that not one participant believed that women were becoming more violent. They all agreed that the increase in the number of women being arrested was due to changes in police training and protocols, such as mandatory arrest, which is where police are required to make an arrest upon probable cause that a crime had been committed. Thus, if there appeared to be both parties who used violence or both parties had injuries, no matter who was responsible, both parties are often arrested. Often the woman would accept a plea to domestic violence so as to go home to their children and prevent them from being taken by Child Protective Services.

Many participants in the Miller (2001) study indicated that men manipulated and had become savvy to the criminal justice system in ways to further harm them. They would use this knowledge to control women, particularly around issues with the children. For example, men would not accept a plea so that, at trial, the women could potentially lose her children or even end up incarcerated. More examples include men inflicting wounds on themselves to have her arrested, men calling 911 before she could, and the men purposely remaining very calm when the officers arrived. The respondents also agreed that it seemed the police granted more weight to the person who called 911. There was overwhelming agreement that the police are not spending enough time fully investigating and understanding the situation. Conversely, the police fear liability if they use their judgment.

The prosecutors identified the issue of bail as a problem for women arrested, as the men are usually able to make bail, whereas the women are typically held. They also found that women are intimidated by the justice system and stigmatized by the consequences, which often include a record, public housing denials, loss of welfare benefits, immigration issues, and custody hearings. These issues are more salient for women as they are often the primary caretakers. Respondents also felt that women were coerced into treatment and confused by the system, in which they did not understand the full implications of a guilty plea. The data reveal that the respondents are aware of the confusion for women when they are arrested for domestic violence.

Also noted was that women seem to use violence differently than men, in which they are usually acting in self-defense or are reacting to abuse in the relationship. Law enforcement and court action would better serve women who are arrested if they understood their violence in a contextual way and not as an isolated incident (Miller 2001).

Interestingly, those women who are being held in jail either pre- or post-adjudication were able to serve time on a domestic violence or substance abuse unit in Broward County Sheriff's Office North Jail. Here, there are special 'life-skills' programs for the women in this unit including a 12-week Survivor Therapy Empowerment Program (STEP) run by Lenore Walker and her Forensic Psychology Practicum team of students (Walker 2009). Although many of the women in these units in general population were not arrested on domestic violence charges, the large percentage of them who have been abuse victims makes them motivated to attend the group treatment trauma-specific program. The analysis of findings from those who have attended over the past 5 years indicates that the program is helpful, particularly in reducing anxiety and providing information to assist the women make better choices when they are released (Walker 2009; Jungersen et al. in press).

Domestic Violence Court for Youth

The growing number of teenagers who are arrested for domestic violence, both in their homes and with their dates, has spawned the idea of a special problem-solving court for them. Juveniles who are arrested for delinquency frequently have a history of having been abused themselves as well as having been exposed to domestic violence. As violence is learned behavior, it is not surprising that they are at high risk to use violence in their own lives. Many of these youth should not be sent back into violent and chaotic homes. They need special services appropriate to their age and psychological development. The TEAMCHILD program at the Broward County Legal Aid identifies many of these youth and attempts to link them with the limited community services available. Placing them in one Domestic Violence Court would assist in referrals and follow-up for those services.

Chapter 4
Competency Restoration Programs

Abstract Competency restoration programs have had various features in common but few are comprehensive in trying to restore or build competency in those people found incompetent to proceed to trial. A model program outline is proposed here.

Introduction

When a criminal defendant is found incompetent to stand trial (i.e., not having a rational or a factual understanding of the trial proceedings and/or not being to assist counsel with a reasonable degree of rational understanding), she or he is committed to a treatment program with the intent of restoring her or him to competency. Approximately 12,000 defendants in the United States are found incompetent to stand trial each year. These treatment programs can be either community-based or inpatient, but most often, they are inpatient. If such competency restoration can be accomplished within a fixed period of time designated by the court, then the defendant will be sent back to court to face subsequent proceedings. If the defendant cannot be restored within a fixed period of time, the treatment facility may ask for more time (which is usually granted by the court), or, in the case of severe mental illness, mental retardation, or organic impairment, the treatment facility may declare the defendant "unrestorable" or "unlikely to regain competency within the foreseeable future." In such cases, the court commences another hearing, pursuant to *Jackson v. Indiana* (406 U.S. 715, 1972) to determine whether or not the defendant meets the criteria for involuntary commitment (danger to self or others by virtue of mental illness). *Jackson v. Indiana* forbade indefinite confinement based on mental condition alone, and stated that continued confinement could only be justified by progress toward the goal of competency.

If the defendant meets these criteria, she or he may then be civilly committed; if the defendant does not meet the criteria, she or he, pursuant to *Jackson v. Indiana*, must be released. While the United States Supreme Court never specified what a "reasonable" period of time for competency restoration was, many states, in their

L.E.A. Walker et al., *Best Practices for the Mentally Ill*
in the Criminal Justice System, SpringerBriefs in Behavioral Criminology,
DOI 10.1007/978-3-319-21656-0_4

own evidence codes, have defined these parameters. Looking just at the law, therefore, a competency restoration program, should at the very least, instruct defendants about areas they need to know to understand court proceedings, treat the underlying mental illness, evaluate the possibility of mental retardation or organic impairment that may make the task more difficult; and, if the defendant does not appear to be responding to treatment, do a risk assessment to determine the defendant's violence potential, in case involuntary commitment proceedings arise.

Unfortunately, all too many competency restoration programs merely teach, by rote learning, the elements of trial competency to defendants, with little regard for treatment of the underlying mental illness, nor any diagnostic procedures to address the other important issues such as retardation or brain impairment. When the defendant seemingly is unable to understand the concepts, she or he is declared to be malingering and sent back to court anyway. In one recent example, an intern reported that the psychologist on the ward said to a patient who was actively hallucinating, "We are not here to talk about your crazy voices; we are here to learn about what goes in court!"

Best practices must incorporate then, not only an understanding of court procedures, but also a treatment program for the underlying mental illness, and comprehensive diagnostic procedures to address the likelihood of success of treatment, and the risk assessment of the potential for future violence. Especially in the case of mentally retarded individuals, they have never been competent, so to use the term "restoration" is really a misnomer. For this group, competence-creating services could better be referred to as education or habilitation. *Jackson v. Indiana,* noted above, required that forensic treatment programs develop effective treatment programs to comply with the limited time periods allowed for restoration.

Competency Restoration needs to include treatment of the underlying mental disorder along with a psychoeducational component that teaches the defendant such issues as knowledge of the charge and its possible consequences, knowledge of courtroom procedure, ability to communicate rationally with one's attorney, and the ability to meaningfully integrate and use these abilities in a trial or other court proceeding (Hoge et al. 1999; Roesch et al. 2006). What follows is a brief discussion of some programs utilized in the past.

Program Overview

One of the first competency restoration programs at Atascadero State Hospital began with an assessment of trial competency based on a structured interview, followed by an individualized treatment plan based on the areas of deficit identified in that instrument. Defendants took a competence education class and participated in a mock trial exercise; this was followed by a formal clinical assessment, which included many of the mental health issues not included in the other modules.

A competency restoration program at a maximum security forensic hospital in Ohio also dealt initially with knowledge of charges and ability to assist counsel, but followed it up with placement in one of five groups with specific treatment programs designed for each. For instance, there would be a group of psychotically confused incompetent defendants where the emphasis would be on treating the psychosis, which interfered with the competency and a group of intellectually limited, where the emphasis would be on discussing competency criteria in very simple terms.

A program in Illinois had a very intensive group didactic focus on elements of trial competency, but did not appear to deal with the underlying mental illnesses as much. In Rhode Island, they attempted to develop a treatment program for those with mental retardation. Five modules were presented in sequential order dealing with pleas and their consequences, role of courtroom personnel, trial and plea bargaining, communication with counsel, and dealing with the stress of court proceedings. Each module was reviewed at least three times. The program deliberately moved from rote knowledge at the beginning to requiring an actual functional use of the components later in the program.

A more recent program conducted at Fort Lauderdale Psychiatric Hospital by Nova Southeastern University forensic psychology students also introduced a trauma-specific component into the competency unit with men demonstrating low functioning ability. Although the STEP program had to be modified to be understood by this population, it proved to be an important addition to their healing (Walker et al. 2013). In addition, a new competency evaluation program has begun with mentally ill immigrants who are in danger of being deported back to their country of origin, often because of entering the U.S. illegally or having pled guilty or served time in prison for a designated felony (Walker et al. 2013). It is anticipated that competency restoration programs may be next as more defendants are found Incompetent to Proceed Trial (ITP).

Toward a Best Practice Model for Competency Restoration

All of these programs have some important elements in them, but none have been truly comprehensive. The model competence restoration program will include as follows:

1. *Systematic Competence Assessment*—Defendants, upon admission, will undergo a comprehensive assessment to determine the specific reasons for the incompetence, be they psychotic and confused thinking, limited intelligence, mood fluctuations, or brain impairment.
2. *Individualized Treatment Program*—Each defendant will have treatment program tailored to her or his specific needs. Deficits identified in the initial assessment will be addressed by specific treatment modalities.
3. *Education*—This will be the didactic component consisting of education surrounding charges, sentencing, plea bargaining, roles of courtroom personnel, the trial process, and understanding evidence.

4. *Anxiety Reduction*—Defendants will be taught anxiety reducing techniques to help them deal with the stress of court proceedings.
5. *Additional Education for Defendants with Limited Intelligence*—If incompetence stems from intellectual deficits, a specific intervention based on the results of an intellectual assessment at the outset will be used here. Didactic material may be reviewed a number of subsequent times in individual sessions to address aspects of the group program that were not well understood by the defendant.
6. *Periodic Reassessment*—Each defendant will be reassessed on at least two occasions, focusing on the individualized treatment modules to see whether progress is being made.
7. *Medication*—For those defendants whose incompetence is based on psychosis or mood disorders, appropriate medications will be prescribed and regularly monitored. Medication reassessment will coincide with the periodic reassessment of competence to see if the pharmacotherapy needs to be altered.
8. *Assessments of Capacity*—A procedure needs to be set in place for the assessment of competency to make treatment decisions, especially when medication is involved. This may vary by depending on relevant statutes and case law.
9. *Risk Assessment*—Considering the fact that some defendants who are unrestorable need to be evaluated for involuntary commitment, there needs to be a standard protocol for assessing risk of future violence using empirically based instruments.

Conclusion

It is understood that these guidelines are limited by current statutes and case law. As these legal standards evolve, they may demand adjustments in the way we think of competency restoration. Regardless, this model represents best practices at this point in time.

There are also several problems involving the point in time at which such competency restoration is undertaken. Even if it is very obvious to all concerned that a given inmate is grossly psychotic, competency restoration cannot be undertaken until such time as the defendant is actually adjudicated ITP by the court. It would be a violation of the defendant's rights to start restoration prior to this finding in court. There is no court order for treatment prior to this time and, therefore, forcing treatment on an individual who is not dangerous prior to adjudication as incompetent has serious constitutional implications. All of the programs described above are hospital-not-jail-based programs, and they occur subsequent to a court finding of ITP. For this reason, mental health treatment initially cannot be based on restoration of competency; it can only be general in nature, to stabilize the mental health of the defendant. Following the adjudication of ITP, competency restoration programs can be started either on a community-based model, or on a forensic hospital model depending on the nature of the offense and the assessment of the potential for violence. Those that can be treated in the community, in a best practices model would be released on bond to follow outpatient treatment; those that need hospitalization would be sent to a forensic hospital, and those that do not need hospitalization, but cannot be released on bond could be seen in jail via a consultative arrangement with various community treatment agencies.

Chapter 5
A Review of Best Practices for the Treatment of Persons with Mental Illness in Jail

Abstract This chapter discusses the need for specific kinds of short-term mental health treatment in jails as opposed to prisons. Although there is a vast amount of information about the treatment of persons with mental illness in prisons where inmates are there for a defined period of time, there is a dearth of literature on treatment in jails where inmates are often unpredictably in and out.

Despite the best attempts to try to assist mentally ill people to stay out of jail, many are not identified initially, refuse to go into treatment, decompensate while in custody, or are considered too dangerous to be released into the community. Therefore, treatment options need to be available for them. There is very little in the literature to determine the best practices for mental health treatment in the jails, especially in the general population. Hiring a mental health supervisor, being prepared to administer and monitor psychotropic medications, and training jail staff to work with the mentally ill are important recommendations in a Best Practices Model (BPM). However, when it comes to psychotherapy or other forms of treatment, there are few models in the literature.

Detainment in a jail is usually short-term and often has no pre-determined limits. Interventions for serious and persistent mental illnesses usually include medication, intensive case management, and sometimes psychotherapy. While some programs have been introduced in prisons, opening up emotional scars while someone is in environments, such as jails, where they have even less free choice, may be counter-productive to treatment goals. Recommended have been medication, short-term psychotherapy with cognitive behavioral goals, therapeutic community-like units for specific problems, such as domestic violence and substance abuse, and individual psychotherapy to assist inmates in recognizing their mental health problems and what can be done about them. There have been some attempts to adapt these types of programs to the jail setting although there is a major problem with defendants in and out of the program due to court hearings and short stays in jail.

Research indicates that persons with mental illness are more likely to be convicted for misdemeanors than persons without mental illness. Moreover, persons with mental illness are incarcerated in jails for a longer duration than persons without mental illness. Risk factors for incarceration include substance use disorders,

© The Author(s) 2016
L.E.A. Walker et al., *Best Practices for the Mentally Ill in the Criminal Justice System*, SpringerBriefs in Behavioral Criminology, DOI 10.1007/978-3-319-21656-0_5

treatment non-compliance, and homelessness. For persons with mental illness incarcerated in jail, recidivism is associated with treatment non-compliance, substance abuse, psychotic symptoms, and residential instability (Lamberti et al. 2001).

County and city jails are currently reframing correctional treatment policy, because they reabsorb the costs of recidivism, processing, retrial, and re-incarceration (Turley et al. 2004). Long-term jail inmates with mental illness often wait months to years before the completion of their case. These persons have a higher potential for causing disruptions and are at a higher risk for victimization (Ruddell 2006). "…Jails become the front-door, first responder to persons with psychiatric impairments, a role most are ill prepared to serve. Although a cheaper temporary response than hospitalization, incarcerating nonviolent offenders with mental illness meets the long-term needs of no stakeholder—the inmate, the justice system, or the community" (Ruddell 2006, p. 119). Although there is a vast amount of information about the treatment of persons with mental illness in prisons where inmates are there for a defined period of time, there is a dearth of literature on treatment in jails where inmates are often unpredictably in and out.

Treatment in Jail

Descriptive Studies

In a study by Ruddell (2006), 134 jails were surveyed representing 39 states covering all regions of the United States. The survey consisted of a list of 12 jail-based strategies and an evaluation of the efficacy of these interventions. The results indicate that reliance on all 12 jail-based interventions was infrequent. Most developed programs and strategies specifically designed to meet the needs and conditions of the community, which included the population of mentally ill inmates, the jail size, and the availability of community or county resources. The strategies rated as most effective were admissions screening (51.5 %) and suicide risk forms (56.8 %); however, only a few jails reported that they did not use these strategies. Mental health training for jail officers (35.6 %), employing mental health case managers (35.1 %), and mental health housing within the jail (32.6 %) were also rated as effective. The strategies rated as least effective were released to mental health treatment (11.5 %), prebooking jail diversion (11.0 %), and post-booking jail diversion (11.0 %). Although mental health units were rated as effective, the author notes that less than half of the facilities had such units. Mental health managers were present in more than 75 % of the jails and 70 % of respondents rated that the managers were very or somewhat effective. The author states that a plausible explanation why diversion programs were rated as least effective is because less than half of the jails reported that their communities had such programs, thus ratings were based on small samples. Limitations of the results include the underrepresentation of small jails and jails in the Northeastern states. Also, the author notes that since the survey was based on ratings of efficacy, there is a lack of empirical evidence to support the ratings (Ruddel 2006).

Current Practice

"Many jails do not provide a comprehensive system of correctional health care due to their small size and brief duration of stay" (Maier et al. 1998, p. 238). Due to the short-term duration of incarceration of persons in jail, current practice utilizes psychotropic medications as the first line of treatment. Other interventions include crisis intervention, which consists of transfer to other units, use of psychotropic medications, observation, and brief psychosocial treatment. It is recommended that treatment consists of daily observation, availability of psychotropic medication, requisite physical health care, and monitoring by psychiatrists (Maier et al. 1998).

Suicide

Suicide in jails is more frequent than in prisons and has a likelihood of nine times greater than in the general population. It has been reported that in jails, more than 50 % of suicides occur within the first month of incarceration (Maier et al. 1998). Essential elements of a suicide prevention program include identification, staff observation, assessment of suicidality, observation of those inmates assessed as potentially suicidal, appropriate housing, and referral to mental health services. Moreover, a comprehensive program should include communication between the treatment team, notification of family members of attempted or completed suicides, and administrative review upon completion of a suicide (Maier et al. 1998). Many of the precautions recommended in best practices for suicide screening and intervention can be applied in the jail setting (Fagan and Ax 2003).

Female Inmates

Research indicates that lifetime prevalence of psychopathology in incarcerated women is higher than the general population. Moreover, incarcerated women are more likely to have a mental illness, with an estimated one-third to two-thirds of all women in correctional settings requiring mental health treatment and one-fifth having a history of taking psychotropic medication. Incarcerated women are likely to have major depressive disorder, posttraumatic stress disorder, and substance abuse and dependence (Lewis 2006). Although the overall prevalence of psychopathology was higher, the prevalence of schizophrenia and panic disorder was not higher than the general population. Moreover, the prevalence of substance abuse and dependence and personality disorders (i.e., antisocial, borderline) was higher than the general population (Lewis 2006; Maier et al. 1998).

Treatment for incarcerated women with mental illness is more likely by psychotropic medication than for men. It has been recommended that treatment in jail should focus on grief and distress, fear of job loss or future job placement, distress from cessation of alcohol or drug use, fear of contracting AIDS, depression, fear of correctional officers, fear of losing control, and fear of sexual assault. Other treatment focuses should be physical health, explanation of their behavior to their family, custody or divorce proceedings during incarceration, fear of reintegration into the community (e.g., relapse, engaging in prior behaviors), and fear of being sent to prison (Maier et al. 1998).

Treatment in Correctional Settings

Individual Treatment

Chaiken et al. (2005) recommend short-term, goal-oriented behavioral, or cognitive interventions. Interventions should identify and educate the patient on available resources in the correctional setting (Chaiken et al. 2005; Maier et al. 1998). Interventions that should not be utilized include regressive interventions that require interpersonal trust, development of insight, and change in coping behavior (Chaiken et al. 2005). Such interventions could be counterproductive due to limitations of treatment duration due to transfer or release.

Cognitive Behavioral Therapy (CBT) has been an intervention utilized in correctional settings. CBT in correctional settings targets "antisocial, socially maladaptive patterns of thinking or behavior rather than disorders that may have a lesser association with criminality or disruption of the milieu" (Chaiken et al. 2005, p. 124). Research indicates that CBT is effective in the treatment of violent inmates with personality disorders and in the combination with social skills training for sexual offenders (Chaiken et al. 2005).

Dialectical Behavior Therapy (DBT) has been shown to reduce self-injurious or violent behaviors in inmates (Chaiken et al. 2005). Current application of DBT in correctional settings utilizes the intervention as an intensive Behavior Therapy. DBT firsts aims to (1) reduce self-injurious or violent behaviors, and then (2) reduce behaviors that interfere with treatment.

Therapeutic communities have been suggested as a means to help inmates play an active role in their treatment. Inmates are encouraged to provide recommendations into program guidelines, rules, and procedures. These meetings facilitate conflict resolution, teach social skills, and help inmates learn prosocial behavior and self-advocacy. Moreover, it is recommended that mental health and custody supervisors are present at the meetings to address the concerns of the inmates (Chaiken et al. 2005).

Behavioral programs, such as behavior incentive programs and token economies, are often-utilized interventions in correctional settings. These interventions aim to change maladaptive behaviors and provide the inmate incentives for presentation of agreed upon behaviors (Chaiken et al. 2005). Behavior therapies, skills teaching, and family therapy are necessary in combination with medication (Rice and Harris 1997). This treatment teaches the inmate the skills to acquire and maintain friends or a job or to live in a community. Contingency management has been efficacious in providing incarcerated persons with psychotic symptoms with the skills necessary to leave the institutional setting and live in a community setting. The treatment focus is on systematically providing positive social and material consequences for independent, prosocial behaviors, while decreasing or eliminating attention for dependent, symptomatic behavior. Research indicates that this treatment is not more costly than available treatments (Rice and Harris 1997).

Behavior therapy in correctional settings consists of two approaches: token economy and specific skills training. Token economies have been shown to be more effective than intensive therapeutic communities. Specific skills training is provided for individuals or small groups of clients. This includes shaping, coaching, modeling, role-playing practice, and feedback. The social skills taught are initiating and maintaining friendships; anger management or aggression replacement; assertion, interpersonal problem solving, and conversation skills; and the management of positive psychotic symptoms (Rice and Harris 1997). Research indicates that a combination of specific skills training, vocational training, and training for families with medication has led to improvement in symptoms, social adjustment, public safety, and happiness. In particular, social skills training has been shown to increase community adjustment, reduce psychotic symptoms, and reduce hospitalizations. Moreover, the effects of treatment have a lasting effect (Rice and Harris 1997).

As previously stated, case management has been an effective means of treatment. However, it has been shown to have little or no effect on quality of life, symptoms, social adjustment, and antisocial behavior. Research has reported conflicting findings on case management's effect on the frequency and duration of hospitalizations. Rice and Harris (1997) reviewed the studies to date and concluded that case management has led to both increases and in reductions in the frequency and duration of hospitalizations. The authors recommended that case managers are assertive and tailor the intensity of the client's social interaction to their ability to handle social stimulation. Moreover, they should use positive reinforcement, minimize rather than enhance professional status, and maintain continued contact for inmates with mental illness.

Group Treatment

Group interventions are recommended in correctional settings due to the benefits of group processing. The group could be used for support, reality testing and feedback, didactic education, improvement of social skills, decreasing isolation, and increasing recreational activities (Chaiken et al. 2005; Maier et al. 1998). In group interventions, the facilitator should be mindful that group therapy may be harmful if the rules and consequences for breaking group rules are not clarified upon initiation of treatment. Essential in group interventions is that the safety of all inmates is considered and all attempts are made to ensure safety. Physical safety can be ensured through room design and by having the facilitator sit closest to the exit. Contingent upon the occurrence of conflict, the facilitator must decide if this could be therapeutic or requires intervention. Moreover, the facilitator must discuss issues of confidentiality with the group and ensure that the group understands that he or she does not have the ability to protect confidentiality. Facilitators should encourage participation and discuss situations where the member should refrain from public disclosure (Chaiken et al. 2005).

Inclusion criteria, according to ethnicity, age, term length, and diagnosis, can be either beneficial or detrimental. Although inclusion based on ethnicity might be a facilitator, it might validate and enhance negative feelings toward other ethnic groups. In some cases, correctional staff may prohibit integrated groups in an effort to prevent violent altercations (Chaiken et al. 2005).

Psychotic Symptoms

As noted by Lovell and Jamelka (1998), "…severe mental disorder resulting in psychotic symptoms is a causal factor in violent crime…it can be controlled by appropriate treatment and supervision…imprisonment without appropriate treatment fails to do so" (p. 57). Treatment for psychotic symptoms of mentally ill inmates includes treatment with antipsychotic drugs and behavior therapy (e.g., behavior modification, psychoeducational treatment, and psychosocial rehabilitation). Clozapine and respiridone have been the effective treatments, but are viewed as a last resort due to their high costs (Rice and Harris 1997). Burns (2005) states that the use of clozapine in correctional settings has been shown to be effective in hospital settings, but has not been replaced the former. For example, in a study of 25 refractory inmates with schizophrenia or schizoaffective disorder in a forensic hospital, the results indicated that the 76 % of those treated with clozapine showed a significant response to treatment, with over 50 % improving. Moreover, the author contends that it is plausible that the results could be generalized to correctional settings (Burns 2005). The cost of newer antipsychotics has been a deterrent from their utilization; however, it has been noted that although they are more expensive, they make significant reductions in psychotic symptoms, resulting in reduced expenses for crisis interventions (Burns 2005; Maier et al. 1998).

Medications that have been shown to be efficacious and cost effective are standard neuroleptics; if the neuroleptic fails, or produces unfavorable side effects, one or two drugs from the same class are utilized. It has been suggested that because unsuccessful treatment and initial side effects are related to medication noncompliance, atypical antipsychotics (e.g., clozapine and respiridone) should be the first choice of treatment.

Anxiety and Depression

Antidepressants, such as paroxetine (Paxil), venlafaxine (Effexor), and nefazodone (Serzone), have been efficacious in the treatment of anxiety disorders (Burns 2005). It has been reported that 19 % of inmates exhibit depressive symptoms of at least moderate severity. However, less than 10 % have a primary diagnosis of a mood disorder and 19 % are on either antidepressants or lithium (Rice and Harris 1997). Pharmacological treatment includes monamine oxidase inhibitors (MAOI), tricyclic antidepressants (TCA), or serotonin reuptake inhibitors (SSRI). Use of MAOI's is not advised due to the rigidity of dietary monitoring necessitated by the drug, the limitation of over-the-counter medications due to synergistic effects, and the availability of medications that are equally efficacious or more effective. Although TCA are inexpensive, they should be considered as treatment contingent upon failure to respond to other antidepressants. TCA have the risk of abuse due to their anticholinergic properties and should be safeguarded. SSRI have been shown to be efficacious and have a lower level of toxicity than MAOI and TCA (Burns 2005). Other psychotropic medications that are recommended include amoxapine (Asendin), bupropion (Wellbutrin), mirtazapine (Remeron), venlafaxine (Effexor), and nefazodone (Serzone). The use of bupropion should be monitored due to reports of inhalation for intoxication (Burns 2005).

Maier et al. (1998) recommend that treatment focus on the process of acculturation to incarceration before treatment for their mood disturbance. The authors recommend psychosocial treatment before treatment with psychotropic mediation, because the use of psychotropics can delay the acculturation process.

Sleep Disturbance

Treatment for sleep disturbance includes low doses of antidepressants due to their sedating effects. Although part of practice, it is advised to not use antidepressants in this form of treatment because this treatment prescribes for side effect rather than target action. Recommended treatments include reduction of caffeine intake, increasing exercise, and use of noise blockers (e.g., ear plugs; Burns 2005).

Aggression Management

A multifaceted approach has been recommended to reduce violence in institutions. Behavior and psychopharmacological interventions should be the treatment for those mentally ill inmates who exhibit frequent violent behavior. Behavioral techniques should provide predetermined consequences for aggressive acts and for prosocial and cooperative behavior. Moreover, they should be supported by Cognitive Behavioral Therapy to teach anger management techniques (Rice et al. 1997). Recommended psychotropic medications include lithium, beta-blockers, carbamazepine, and clozapine (Maier et al. 1998).

Rice and Harris (1997) believe that institutional violence is not solely the product of pathology, but is the result of the interaction between the mentally ill offender and the institutional staff. A five-day staff training course has been shown to reduce assaults, lower staff workdays lost due to injuries caused by a mentally ill offender, improve ward morale, increase staff ratings of their own effectiveness, and increase ratings of self-esteem by the mentally ill offender. This program includes early recognition of pathology, early verbal intervention to defuse aggressive behavior, and safe and effective techniques for manual restraint and self-defense.

Female Inmates

As noted by Lewis (2006), the treatment of women in correctional settings must be differentiated from treatment of males. Incarcerated women are more likely to have a history of victimization and are at risk for future victimization. There is some literature indicating that some might re-enact their victimization through sexual behavior with staff, although reports of staff sexual harassment and abuse with inmates are not uncommon. It is recommended that staff receive training on sexual misconduct, issues of confidentiality, and procedures for immediately reporting sexual misconduct (Lewis 2006). Due to the high prevalence of comorbidity, trauma treatment should be integrated with treatment for substance use disorders. Moreover, treatment should emphasis the development of skills to foster appropriate relationships (Jungersen et al. in press; Lewis 2006; Walker 2009).

Case management and therapeutic communities are two recommended interventions. Case managers serve as a liaison for the inmate's mental and physical health, as well as programming needs and vocation assistance. Therapeutic communities would serve to foster relationships, facilitate communication, increase community involvement, and provide agency and empowerment (Lewis 2006).

Sex Offenders

Available treatments for sex offenders include non-behavioral psychotherapy, psychopharmacological treatment, and behavior or cognitive-behavioral therapy. The most common treatment for incarcerated persons who commit sex crimes against children and rape is individual or group psychotherapy. However, research indicates that this form of treatment is not effective in reducing the likelihood of future sex offending. Moreover, humanistic and psychodynamic treatments have also proven to be ineffective in stopping sex offenses (Rice and Harris 1997). Psychopharmacological treatment includes the use of cyproterone acetate (CPA) and medroxyprogesterone (MPA). Both CPA and MPA reduce testosterone levels and lead to reduction in sexual arousal, but the relationship between the medications and arousal is not perfect. The side effects of both medications include weight gain, fatigue, headaches, reduced body hair, depression, and gastrointestinal problems. Research indicates that there is low medication adherence, but for those who continue, there is a reduction of re-offense rates (Rice and Harris 1997). It is unusual for those accused of sexual offenses to be given treatment in the jail or prison, although there are a few reported programs in prison that have some limited success. In many states, there are sexual predator laws that cause a convicted sex offender to be held in civil court for treatment until such time they are no longer considered dangerous.

Recidivism

Some research indicates that although mental illness may be the cause of some violent behavior, there are no differences between persons with mental illness who are incarcerated and those persons incarcerated without mental illness (Lovell et al. 1998). As noted by Dvoskin and Patterson (1998), public perception of persons with mental illness who upon release re-offend, is that they are dangerous. The community expects that upon release these persons are "fixed," but devoid in their expectation is that these persons need progressive transition into the community (p. 3). It has been recommended that the best practice for reintegration is to progressively decrease structure, while increasing freedom and responsibility (Dvoskin et al. 1998; Maier and Fulton 1998).

Treatment recommendations for reducing criminal propensity rely on three principles: risk, need, and responsivity. Intensive supervision should be reserved for high-risk cases and minimal service should be provided to low-risk cases. Treatment to reduce recidivism must address factors that are changeable and empirically related to criminal conduct. Treatment targets should include changing antisocial attitudes and peer associations, reducing substance dependency, promoting identification with prosocial role models, developing prosocial skills, and increasing self-control and self-management skills. Moreover, mentally ill offenders are most responsive to practitioners who use behavioral and social learning principles delivered in a "fair but firm" approach and who model and reward prosocial thinking, feeling, and acting (Rice and Harris 1997, p. 144); if followed, they estimated that effective treatment could reduce recidivism by 50 %.

Model Programs

One application of behavioral interventions is the Intensive Behavior Unit (IBTU), which is utilized for incarcerated persons with mental illness who have not adjusted to prison rules and regulations. In a study by Daniel et al. (2003), IBTU was utilized in a maximum-security female prison. Admission criteria included behaviors that were disturbing to the prison population, a history of antisocial behavior, and inability to participate in the programmed activities offered by the institution. The program monitored personal hygiene and prosocial behaviors. Upon admission, inmates were allowed one phone call per month and 1 h of recreation between Monday and Friday. Also, there were no visitation or store privileges allowed and the inmate was restricted to their room. After a period of behavior stabilization of 3 weeks, the inmate progressed to the next level where they were restricted to the unit, allotted 15 min of telephone time, and allowed 2 h of television. Upon a period of behavior stability, the inmate was reintegrated with the general prison population. If the inmate exhibited any antisocial behavior, they were placed in a lower level of privilege. The results indicated that there was significant difference between behavior reports prior to admission to the unit as compared to 3 months after release (Daniel 2003).

The North Broward Detention Center (NBDC), one of the five facilities operated by the Broward Sheriff's Office (BSO), has a 375 bed Mental Health Unit located there along with 700 other general population inmates. The Mental Health Unit is separated into 12 open mental health units, 23 closed mental health units, and special observation units. The NBDC also includes a male and a female infirmary and a MRSA unit. Psychological services offered in the mental health units include both psychiatric and psychological services such as medication management, psychological testing, suicide prevention, crisis intervention, individual and group therapy, video programming, and discharge planning.

The staff in the Mental Health Units consists of psychiatrists, psychologists, psychology interns, mental health specialists, social workers, registered nurses, and health educators. In addition to those services, religious services, General Education classes, and 12-Step meetings are offered. The overall mission of the Mental Health Unit is to provide services to inmates with mental illness in order to assist them in their adjustment to the correctional setting. Within a safe and secure environment, those services incorporate individual therapy, psychological assessments, release/discharge planning, deputy training, psycho-education, and psycho-social group programs.

BSO also has an In Custody Program Unit, which consists of court ordered and volunteer participants for males and females. Program components include Substance Abuse (30–60 days), Anger Management and Domestic Violence (60 days), Life Skills (60 days) (eclectic), and Basic Computer Skills (60 days). The format is usually up to 60 days in a unit or a series of workshops in a particular subject area held for general population inmates in a designated program area. All in-unit programs and facilities have auxiliary programs and access to approved community agencies (e.g., N.A., A.A., Al Anon, Positive Images, Work Force One).

Interestingly, battered women and other trauma victims, who have volunteered to attend the 12-unit Survivor Therapy Empowerment Program (STEP) program facilitated by NSU Forensic Psychology doctoral students, reported that they have found the time they spend on the special units (Domestic Violence and Substance Units in 2008) therapeutic and educational, providing a calm atmosphere away from the chaos of their lives. Assessment indicated that many of these women had high levels of anxiety, emotional reliance on others, and difficulty with self-esteem although not usually problems with assertiveness. In the 8 years that STEP has been provided to the women in jail, approximately 40 women each day attend as many of the 12 weekly sessions as they can, given their court schedules. One of the co-authors (Walker) was the supervisor of the STEP program, and learned that conducting this type of group in a jail setting required many accommodations including making sure each session of the 12 units provided in the program stood on its own as it was impossible to know if a participant would be there the next time, mostly due to jail and court scheduling conflicts. As was mentioned in the prior chapter, a similar group is offered in the hospital for those adjudicated incompetent to proceed to trial and now it has been adopted in the jail clinic for men and women, and at NSU's outpatient Family Violence Program so that a seamless transition is available to deal with trauma when defendants are discharged into the community. This program was assessed for outcomes and found to reduce anxiety, levels in dose-related manner. That is, the more sessions attended, the more effective the treatment (Jungersen et al. in press).

Treatment Considerations and Recommendations

Treatment in correctional settings presents impediments toward recovery that are not experienced in other clinical settings. Essential to the therapeutic process is the development of rapport, which may be a difficult process in correctional settings (Chaiken et al. 2005). Correctional settings create a somewhat adversarial environment whereby inmates perceive all non-inmates as persons of authority and control. As noted by Chaiken et al. (2005), rapport is accomplished over time through empathy, discussion of boundaries, defining goals of treatment, and through the consistency of treatment. The practitioner should identify impediments toward the establishment of rapport, as well as positive factors (e.g., motivation, personality traits, and beliefs in the efficacy of the therapeutic process).

Available settings to provide individual treatment present novel impediments to the therapeutic process, as well as ethical questions, such as confidentiality and safety. Inmates may have reluctance for disclosure if the therapeutic setting is their housing unit, due to the ability of other inmates to hear the conversation. Kupers (2001) makes an office the minimal requirement for conducting treatment sessions.

Due to the perception of non-inmates as adversarial, one of the first tasks of the practitioner should be to differentiate him or herself from the custody staff (Chaiken et al. 2005; Kupers 2001; Maier and Fulton 1998). The practitioner should be cautious in balancing the establishment of rapport and boundaries to ensure that there are no legal or ethical violations (Chaiken et al. 2005). Moreover, the practitioner must develop skills that emphasize setting limits without being punitive (Chaiken et al. 2005).

As noted by Dvoskin and Patterson (1998), treatment should focus on teaching the inmate to manage his or her symptoms, identification of high-risk situations, and training in necessary skills for community living. Treatment should include increasing support systems and intensive case management for inmates with a history of violent behavior. Moreover, it is important to address the inmate's defensiveness toward their behavior (Maier and Fulton 1998).

In correctional settings, the utilization of interdisciplinary teams is essential in providing the best quality of treatment for the inmate (Chaiken et al. 2005; Dvoskin and Patterson 1998). The interdisciplinary team focuses on facilitating relations and communication between psychiatrists, psychologists, social workers, primary care physicians, nurses, psychiatric technicians, recreational therapists, custody staff, and any other staff who are in contact with the inmate (Chaiken et al. 2005). Moreover, treatment teams should focus on those with serious mental illness, as well as destructive, disruptive, assaultive, or self-injurious behaviors (Clark 2004). Essential to providing the best quality of care is corroboration on clearly defined goals and utilization of the training and expertise of each constituent of the team. Teams should meet to not only discuss the progress of treatment, but to resolve conflicts due to theoretical orientation.

Dvoskin and Patterson (1998) have recommended a direct care staff-to-inmate ratio of 1.6:1. In a survey conducted in 1989, results indicated that the national mean of direct care staff-to-inmate ratio was 1.3, ranging from 0.35 to 4.0. Moreover, the authors provide the following recommendation for a 24-bed ward in a psychiatric hospital: one Treatment team leader; one Psychiatrist; one Ph.D. or Psy.D. clinical psychologist; one Master's level social worker; five Registered nurses; two Clinical nurses; 20 Treatment/security assistants; 2.5 Treatment security supervisors; four Activity therapists; and one Teacher.

In correctional settings with psychiatric units, it is recommended that the inmate should become involved in their treatment. The development of the treatment plan should be a collaborative process, acknowledging that the treatment team will be utilized to its full extent (Maier et al. 1998). If the inmate should refuse to enter into treatment, it is recommended that the treatment plan be renamed and conceptualized as a management plan. Those in the management and treatment plan would have access to all resources, as well as interaction with the treatment team. The difference between groups is that those in the treatment plan will receive treatment that is congruent with their treatment goals.

Those in the management plan will be in a treatment program designed toward management of their behavior within the unit (Maier and Fulton 1998). Moreover, those in the management plan must agree to abide to the policies and procedures of the unit, to not be a disruption to the treatment of others, and to agree that non-compliance with the policies and procedures will result in sanctions or transfer to other housing units. As previously mentioned, the treatment of mentally ill in correctional settings requires multidisciplinary treatment. A model program should consist of a crisis intervention program, an acute care program, and a chronic care program. Moreover, treatment should include outpatient treatment services, consultation services, and release or transfer planning (Maier and Fulton 1998).

Past treatment with psychotropic medications has utilized antipsychotics as a means of management for "undesirable behavior" (Burns 2005). Current practice recommends the use of treatment algorithms, which specify the types of medications to be used, dosage levels, and guidelines for altering medication dosages or type of medication. The use of benzodiazepines is strongly discouraged in correctional settings, due to their likelihood for abuse and criminal activity (e.g., purchasing, stealing, and physical altercations). Benzodiazepines should solely be utilized for medical detoxification or prevention of withdrawal symptoms (Burns 2005).

Burns (2005) makes several recommendations for the prescription of psychotropic medication as well as recommendations for correctional administration. It is recommended that prescribers are familiar with the correctional facility's medication procedures. Prescribers should be familiar with environmental risks and provide education to the inmates and medical and security staff on the risks. It is recommended that clinical decisions be determined on evidence-based treatment guidelines or medical algorithms. Correctional administration should utilize representation medications from antipsychotics, antidepressants, and mood-stabilizers. Moreover, access should be provided to other psychotropic medications to ensure appropriate treatment (Burns 2005).

In a best practices approach, treatment should focus on teaching the inmate to manage his or her symptoms, identification of high-risk situations, and training in necessary skills for community living. It should include increasing support systems and intense case management for inmates with a history of violent behavior. Jails should attempt to minimize the length of stay of mentally ill inmates, provide a safe and secure environment, address the inmate's physical and psychological needs, and establish treatment plans that bridge mental health services and the jail (Ruddell 2006). Traditional diagnostic approaches are of limited value when determining appropriate treatments for mentally ill offenders. It is recommended that direct approaches that determine the cognitive, behavioral, and psychosocial strengths and weaknesses of mentally ill offenders will be the most effective in determining treatment (Rice and Harris 1997). Lovell and Jemelka (1998) cogently state that the treatment of persons with mental illness in correctional settings will lead to reductions in costs associated with their behavior.

Chapter 6
Conclusions and Recommendations

Abstract This chapter presents the results of the survey of community stake-holders and integrates them together with the literature reviews to formulate final recommendations for a BPM.

In conclusion, the Best Practices Model (BPM) was identified by the literature and integrated with common practices in community policing, to keep the mentally ill out of the jails wherever possible. If it is not possible, then the next step is to send people to specialty or problem-solving courts, or use therapeutic jurisprudence (TJ), where those justice-involved individuals have the ability to obtain treatment rather than punishment for their behavior, provided this does not compromise the safety of the community. For those who are declared incompetent to proceed to trial, appropriate competency restoration with psychotherapy and medication, where necessary, may help restore competency, although it must be noted that research suggests the average competency is only restored for one year or less in less than half of those who are declared incompetent. Without this BPM, many of the undertreated mentally ill in jail, even if they make it through their trial, will decompensate once again, if they are sentenced to prison. Finally, jails can and should provide mental health treatment for those in custody including special population, housed in the clinic, and those who receive services in other types of special housing or general population units.

We propose the following recommendations based on our literature review and study with community stakeholders.

1. The Best Practices Model identified in each section of this book should be adopted by the relevant mental health and criminal justice agencies. Even if all parts cannot be implemented immediately, it is in the best interests of the community to develop a plan phasing in to provide appropriate mental health services for those who are forensically involved and mentally ill.
2. It is in the interest of all jurisdictions to train as many law enforcement officers as possible in the CIT model so that the mentally ill are recognized, properly handled, and referred for treatment rather than arrested if they commit a non-violent criminal act during a period of destabilization. It is common for the seriously mentally ill to go off their medication, hoping they will no longer

© The Author(s) 2016
L.E.A. Walker et al., *Best Practices for the Mentally Ill
in the Criminal Justice System*, SpringerBriefs in Behavioral Criminology,
DOI 10.1007/978-3-319-21656-0_6

have to suffer the adverse side effect; however, this is often followed by destabilization. Other situational factors including trauma may also cause destabilization.

3. The number of available beds in receiving facilities for involuntary commitment should be increased to meet the community need. Better collaboration between forensic and non-forensic treatment providers would assist in reaching best practices. For example, it is a common practice for agencies to develop formularies for medication; it would be helpful for agencies who share clients to offer the same formularies so there is no gap in being properly medicated.

4. A coordinating effort should be developed that will provide easy access to the various community services for forensic and non-forensic clients. This addresses the comments made by the community interviewees and judges indicating that they were not always aware of available services for a given client at a specific time. A dynamic database system that is maintained jointly by the social services and the corrections divisions is needed. Ways to overcome the privacy regulations established by HIPAA and other laws will need to be found in order to solve this problem.

5. The forensic treatment providers in the community should get to know what is available in the jail so that they can all deliver similar services with continuity to those who are mentally ill and in and out of jail and the community.

6. The community-based treatment program providers should be supported to integrate forensic clients with their non-forensic clients. Our investigation suggests that the same client may move back and forth between the jail and the community.

7. A Task Force with all the stakeholders and chaired by a well-known and formidable figure like a Judge may be an appropriate venue to coordinate further integration between treatment providers within the courts, jails, and community providers who all work with the same clients. Priorities may be developed so that services can be added in a thoughtful and planned way.

8. The specialty courts, including Mental Health, Drug, and Domestic Violence Courts, are providing a major service to the forensically mentally ill on very limited budgets. They are an integral part of the Best Practices Model and should continue to work well with the community, court, and jail programs.

9. Special programs for women need to be developed in the community so that women who are being arrested and housed in the jails can obtain community-based treatment when released. This is especially needed for substance abusers who have been physically or sexually traumatized. While we found programs for domestic violence and sexual assault victims in the community, when they were also for mentally ill and/or substance abusers, there were insufficient numbers and limited services. Furthermore, many domestic violence and sexual assault programs do not provide trauma-specific therapy.

10. The recommendations of the problem-solving court judges to begin similar courts for juveniles should be acted on. Some communities have already started a Juvenile Drug Court, but most still do not have special courts for mentally ill or trauma victims in their teens. Although we did not conduct a complete

evaluation of the mental health services in the juvenile justice system, the frequent mention of the inadequate services for delinquent adolescents who are substance abusers, mentally ill, or involved in domestic violence suggests that it would be an appropriate preventive strategy to pay attention to these youth before they turn 18 and enter the adult system. Dependency courts are trying to pay attention to the youth under their care prior to their aging out, but this is not well integrated with the adult specialty courts. Indeed, the presence of a significant number of adolescents who are waived into adult court for committing serious felonies suggests that this is a problem that needs to be addressed by law enforcement and the community so that the youth who are mentally ill are provided with adequate services.

11. One of the issues that we were originally asked to comment upon was the possibility of law enforcement building a special needs jail for mental health defendants when a new jail becomes needed. We studied this possibility looking towards the literature and discussing the issue with our interviewees from the community. In support of the creation of a special needs jail, were those who commented on the inadequacy of the physical plant of a typical jail for being able to conduct psychotherapy and other intervention programs, especially groups on each unit. Indeed, we also have tried to run programs in the general population; and although the new jail units are modern state-of-the art, the facilities are inadequate with too few therapy rooms directly on the units. There are also too few staff for the numbers of inmates who want to attend therapy and psychotherapeutic programs. This mirrors the situation in the community where there are more people who want to attend programs than can get to them for a variety of reasons.

Having everyone who needs services in one place as a somewhat captive audience in the jail may be beneficial, given the sporadic program attendance when they are in the community. Although prisons have been able to create adequate space and safety for conducting mental health programs, we could not find any literature where it has been done in a jail. However, given the innovation that many jails have already demonstrated, the lack of precedent should not deter the community from pursuing this course if it is deemed needed. Most of the community stakeholders interviewed supported the building of a mental health jail. At the same time, it would be imperative to make sure that a treatment jail should not become a "dumping ground" for those who already underserved within the community. The potential to create another state hospital rather than a vibrant innovative treatment center is a major deterrent.

In Broward County, Florida, both Judge Lerner-Wren and the elected Public Court Defender Howard Finkelstein are not supportive of a mental health jail for these and other reasons. Both are strong supporters of permitting people to have choice of whether or not to obtain treatment. The National Alliance for the Mentally Ill (NAMI) also believes that it is an individual's choice whether or not to seek treatment and thus, it should not be mandated by the court system. There is also the fear that being housed in a mental health jail will add further to the stigma of being arrested. Therefore, while we do not take a position on this issue, we can recommend that if it is decided to go forward with the project, the above cautions should be met and there should be a seamless transition from the community programs to the jail and back to the community with those defendants who need the services.

Appendix A
Stakeholder Interview Questions

Stakeholder Interview Questions

1. What is your name?
2. What organization do you work for and what is your position?
3. What are the needs of the mentally ill in Broward?
4. Does your organization adhere to what are considered to be best practices?
5. What are the gaps in services you have identified?
6. Does your organization use the GAIN center or the Consensus project websites for information and/or program development?
7. What are your views on the big picture relative to the mentally ill and the judicial system?
8. What areas do you see that need improvement? What are your suggestions?
9. What are the limitations to services that you are aware of, e.g., financial, personnel, referrals, community connections?
10. How do you stay informed of best practices?
11. What do you consider to be the best practice for the service needs related to pre-incarceration, diversion, incarceration, and release?
12. What are your funding sources?
13. Do you perceive your agency in need of training? Who trains your organization's employees?
14. What type of contact do you have with the mental health court, Drug Court, and domestic violence court?
15. What other organizations/programs do you interface with in the community? What is this process like? Is it effective?
16. What are your outcome measures? Do you report them to a governing body?
17. Does your organization have any accreditations? Do you believe such accreditations are an important component?
18. What types of services does your organization provide, e.g., case management, therapy, medication management, and housing?
19. Are their any language barriers that your organization has to attend to when delivering services, if so what are your solutions?
20. What are your thoughts about having a separate facility for mentally ill offenders?

© The Author(s) 2016
L.E.A. Walker et al., *Best Practices for the Mentally Ill in the Criminal Justice System*, SpringerBriefs in Behavioral Criminology, DOI 10.1007/978-3-319-21656-0

21. What is your opinion about the CJS model and how it relates to handling the mentally ill?
22. What is your opinion about whether female clients should receive specialized treatment?

The following questions will be asked to participants when relevant:

23. Describe your follow-up care.
24. What is your agency's recidivism rate?
25. Who do you contact when clients get into legal and/or financial trouble?
26. What type of youth services does the jail provide?
27. What types of programs are offered, e.g., therapy, group, assessment, discharge planning?
28. What is your selection criterion?
29. What are your competency restoration procedures?
30. What are the limitations to providing effective programming?
31. Should clients who are court-ordered into competency restoration training also be ordered into therapy?
32. Do your therapists have adequate contact with the judge who ordered the client into treatment?
33. Does your agency have sufficient resources to serve clients who are court ordered into treatment?
34. Does your agency have sufficient residential treatment beds?
35. Does your agency have sufficient dual diagnosis services?
36. Does your agency have sufficient therapists who speak the client's preferred language?
37. Does your agency have sufficient training in working with women who are trauma victims?
38. Does your agency provide services to domestic violence perpetrators?
39. Does your agency provide services to domestic violence victims?
40. Does your agency provide services to rape victims?

Appendix B
Survey Instrument

Needs Assessment Survey

Please select only 1 answer in relation to each of the following items below.

	Strongly Agree	Agree	Neutral	Disagree	Strongly Disagree
1. Housing for the mentally ill in Broward County is adequate.	SA	A	N	D	SD
2. Clients who are court-ordered into competency restoration programs should be ordered into some form of individual therapy to address their mental illness and life stressors.	SA	A	N	D	SD
3. Clients usually have a sufficient amount of contact with the judge who ordered them into treatment to adequately provide comprehensive wrap around services.	SA	A	N	D	SD
4. Therapists usually have a sufficient amount of contact with the judge who ordered their clients into treatment to adequately provide comprehensive wrap around services.	SA	A	N	D	SD
5. There are sufficient community resources to serve clients who are court ordered into treatment.	SA	A	N	D	SD
6. Broward County has a sufficient number of residential treatment beds to accommodating the growing number of mentally ill residents and court ordered clients.	SA	A	N	D	SD
7. Broward County has a sufficient number of organizations and/or programs that treat and have the capacity to treat the growing number of dually diagnosed clients.	SA	A	N	D	SD
8. There are adequate dual diagnosis services appropriate for court ordered clients.	SA	A	N	D	SD
9. Broward County mental health agencies have the appropriate number of personnel who speak Spanish and Haitian-Creole populations.	SA	A	N	D	SD
10. Training that specializes in working with women/children who have been victims of trauma and/or domestic violence is accessible in Broward County.	SA	A	N	D	SD
11. Broward County has adequate services for the treatment of domestic violence perpetrators.	SA	A	N	D	SD
12. Female clients who have a mental illness should receive specialized treatment.	SA	A	N	D	SD
13. Domestic violence clients who have a mental illness should receive specialized treatment.	SA	A	N	D	SD
14. Broward County has adequate services to treat rape victims and their families.	SA	A	N	D	SD

Additional comments:

_____
_____
_____
_____
_____

L.E.A. Walker et al., *Best Practices for the Mentally Ill in the Criminal Justice System*, SpringerBriefs in Behavioral Criminology, DOI 10.1007/978-3-319-21656-0

Appendix C
Survey Instrument Descriptive Results

BSO Needs Assessment Survey

Question	X	SD	n
1. Housing for the mentally ill in Broward County is adequate.	4.64	0.799	22
2. Clients who are court-ordered into competency restoration programs should be ordered into some form of individual therapy to address their mental illness and life stressors.	2.10	1.20	20
3. The client and therapist have a sufficient amount of contact with the judge who ordered the client into treatment to adequately provide comprehensive wrap around services.	3.71	1.27	14
4. There are sufficient community resources to serve clients who are court ordered into treatment.	4.57	0.60	21
5. Broward County has a sufficient number of residential treatment beds to accommodating the growing number of mentally ill residents and court ordered clients.	4.55	0.69	20
6. Broward County has a sufficient number of organizations and/or programs that treat and have the capacity to treat the growing number of dually diagnosed clients.	3.85	1.04	20
7. There are adequate dual diagnosis services appropriate for court ordered clients.	4.30	0.86	20
8. Broward County mental health agencies have the appropriate number of personnel who speak Spanish and Haitian-Creole populations.	3.76	0.66	17
9. Training that specializes in working with women/children who have been victims of trauma and/or domestic violence is accessible in Broward County.	2.80	1.08	15
10. Broward County has adequate services for the treatment of domestic violence perpetrators.	3.60	0.63	15
11. Female clients should receive specialized treatment.	2.13	0.6	16
12. Broward County has adequate services to treat rape victims and their families.	3.29	0.69	17

© The Author(s) 2016
L.E.A. Walker et al., *Best Practices for the Mentally Ill in the Criminal Justice System*, SpringerBriefs in Behavioral Criminology, DOI 10.1007/978-3-319-21656-0

Bibliography

Bancroft, L. R., & Silverman, J. G. (2002). *The batterer as parent: Addressing the impact of domestic violence on family dynamics*. Thousand Oaks, CA: Sage.

Berman, G. (2004). Redefining criminal courts: Problem-solving and the meaning of justice. *The American Criminal Law Review, 41*(3).

Boccaccini, M. T., Christy, A., Poythress, N., & Kershaw, D. (2005). Rediversion in two postbooking jail diversion programs in Florida. *Psychiatric Services, 56*(7), 835–839.

Boothroyd, R. A., Mercado, C. C., Poythress, N. G., Christy, A., & Petrila, J. (2005). Clinical outcomes of defendants in Mental Health Court. *Psychiatric Services, 56*(7), 829–834.

Boothroyd, R. A., Poythress, N. G., McGaha, A., & Petrila, J. (2003). The Broward Mental Health Court: Process, outcomes, and service utilization. *International Journal of Law and Psychiatry, 26*, 55–71.

Borum, R. (2000). Improving high-risk encounters between people with mental illness and the police. *The Journal of the American Academy of Psychiatry and the Law, 28*, 332–337.

Borum, R., Swanson, J., Swartz, M., & Hiday, V. (1997). Substance abuse, violent behavior and police encounters among persons with severe mental disorder. *Journal of Contemporary Criminal Justice, 13*, 236–250.

Borum, R., Deane, M. W., Steadman, H. J., & Morrissey, J. (1998). Police perspectives on responding to mentally ill people in crisis: Perceptions of program effectiveness. *Behavioral Sciences and the Law, 16*, 393–405.

Bouffard, J., & Taxman, F. (2004). Looking inside the "black box" of Drug Court treatment services using direct observations. *Journal of Drug Issues, 34*(1), 195–218.

Braithwaite, J. (1989). *Crime, shame, and reintegration*. New York: Cambridge University Press.

Brewster, M. P. (2001). An evaluation of the Chester County (PA) Drug Court Program. *Journal of Drug Issues, 31*(1), 177–206.

Bureau of Justice Assistance. (1994). *Understanding community policing: A framework for action*. Washington DC: Author.

Burns, S. L., & Peyrot, M. (2003). Tough love: Nurturing and coercing responsibility and recovery in California Drug Courts. *Social Problems, 50*(3), 416–438.

Burns, K. A. (2005). Psychopharmacology in correctional settings. In C. L. Scott & J. B. Gerbasi (Eds.), *Handbook of correctional mental health* (pp. 89–108). Arlington, VA: American Psychiatric Publishing Inc.

Casey, P. A., & Rottman, D. B. (2005). Problem solving Courts: Models and trends. *Justice System Journal, 26*(1), 35–56.

Casey, R., Berkman, M., Stover, C., Gill, K., Durso, S., & Marans, S. (2007). Preliminary results of a police-advocate home-visit intervention project for victims of domestic violence. *Journal of Aggression, Maltreatment, and Trauma* (In press).

Chaiken, S. B., Thompson, C. R., & Shoemaker, W. E. (2005). Mental health interventions in correctional settings. In C. L. Scott & J. B. Gerbasi (Eds.), *Handbook of correctional mental health* (pp. 109–131). Arlington, VA: American Psychiatric Publishing Inc.

© The Author(s) 2016

L.E.A. Walker et al., *Best Practices for the Mentally Ill in the Criminal Justice System*, SpringerBriefs in Behavioral Criminology,
DOI 10.1007/978-3-319-21656-0

Chesler, P. (2013). *Can "good enough mothers" lose custody of their children to violent and abusive men?*

Christy, A. C., Poythress, N. G., Boothroyd, R. A., Petrila, J., & Mehra, S. (2005). Evaluating the efficiency and community safety goals of the Broward County Mental Health Court. *Behavioral Sciences and the Law, 23,* 1–17.

Clark, J. (2004). *Non-specialty first appearance court models for diverting persons with mental illness: Alternatives to Mental Health Courts.* Delmar, NY: Technical Assistance and Policy Analysis Center for Jail Diversion.

Cochran, C. K., Bernstein, M. S., Coker, K. L., & Walker, L. E. (2005, August). Magistrate court detainee psychosocial characteristics: Implications for mentally ill offenders. In L.E. Walker (Chair), *Forensics for the independent practitioner.* Symposium conducted at the meeting of the American Psychological Association, Washington, D.C.

Compton, M. T., Esterberg, M. L., McGee, R., Kotwicki, R. J., & Oliva, J. R. (2006). Crisis intervention team training: Changes in knowledge, attitudes, and stigma related to schizophrenia. *Psychiatric Services, 57,* 1199–1202.

Cordner, G. W. (2000). A community policing approach to persons with mental illness. *The Journal of the American Academy of Psychiatry and the Law, 28,* 326–331.

Cordner, G. W. (2006). People with mental illness. *U.S. Department of Justice: Problem-oriented guides for police problem-specific guides series, No. 40.*

Crank, J. P. (1994). State theory, myths of policing, and responses to crime. *Law & Society Review, 28,* 325–351.

Cresswell, L. S., & Deschenes, E. P. (2001). Minority and non-minority perceptions of drug court program severity and effectiveness. *Journal of Drug Issues, 31*(1), 259–292.

Cumming, E., Cumming, I., & Edell, L. (1965). Policeman as philosopher, guide, and friend. *Social Problems, 12,* 276–286.

Dalton, B. (2001). Batterer characteristics and treatment completion. *Journal of Interperonal Violence, 16*(12), 1223–1238.

Daniel, C., Jackson, J., & Watkins, J. (2003). Utility of an intensive behavior therapy in a maximum security female prison. *The Behavior Therapist, 26*(1), 211–212.

Dauphnot, L. (1996). The efficacy of community correctional supervisions for offenders with severe mental illness. Doctoral Dissertation, department of psychology, University of Texas at Austin.

Deane, M., Steadman, H., Borum, R., Vesey, B., & Morrissey, J. (1998). Emerging Partnerships between mental health and law enforcement. *Psychiatric Services, 50,* 99–101.

Denckla, D., & Berman, G. (2001). *Rethinking the revolving door: A look at mental illness in the Courts.* Center for Court Innovation: New York, NY.

Ditton, P. M. (1999, July 1). Mental health and treatment of inmates and probationers. *Bureau of Justice Statistics. Special report.* Retrieved June 2008 from www.opj.usdoj.gov/bjs/abstract/mhtip.htm.

Dobash, R. E., & Dobash, R. P. (2000). Evaluating criminal justice interventions for domestic violence. *Crime and Delinquency, 46*(2), 252–270.

Dupont, R., & Cochran, S. (2000). Police response to mental health emergencies: Barriers to change. *The Journal of the American Academy of Psychiatry and the Law, 28,* 338–344.

Dvoskin, J. A., & Patterson, R. F. (1998). Administration of treatment programs for offenders with mental disorders. In R. M. Weinstein (Ed.), *Treatment of offenders with mental disorders* (pp. 1–43). New York, NY: The Guilford Press.

Fagan, T. J., & Ax, R. K. (Eds.). (2003). *Correctional mental health handbook.* Thousand Oaks, CA: Sage.

Feder, L., & Dugan, L. (2004). Testing a court-mandated treatment program for domestic violence offenders: The Broward experiment. National Institute of Justice, Office of Justice Programs, *U.S. Department of Justice, NCJ 199729,* III-14-3-III-14-15.

Felitti, V. J. (2001). Reverse alchemy in childhood: Turning gold into lead. *Health Alert, 8,* 1–4.

Fields, M. D. (2010, February/March). Diversion of domestic violence cases endangers victims. *Domestic Violence Report*, pp. 33–38.

Fisher, W. H., Roy-Bujnowski, K. M., Grudzinskas, A. J., Clayfield, J. C., Banks, S. M., & Wolff, N. (2006). Patterns and prevalence of arrest in a statewide cohort of mental health care consumers. *Psychiatric Services, 57*(11), 1623–1628.

Gainey, R. R., Steen, S., & Engen, R. L. (2005). Exercising options: An assessment of the use of alternative sanctions for drug offenders. *Justice Quarterly, 22*(4).

Gainey, R. R., Steen, S., & Engen, R. L. (2005). Exercising options: An assessment of the use of alternative sanctions for drug offenders. *Justice Quarterly, 22*(4).

Gray, A. R., & Saum, C. A. (2005). Mental health, gender, and drug court completion. *American Journal of Criminal Justice, 33*(1), 55–69.

Gill, K. (2006). *Court model and procedure gathered from secretary chair position of the Greater New Haven Domestic Violence Task Force*. Unpublished.

Goetz, B., & Mitchell, R. E. (2006). Pre-arrest/booking arrest drug control strategies: Diversion to treatment, harm reduction, and police involvement. *Contemporary Drug Problems, 33*(3).

Goldkamp, J. S., & Irons-Guynn, C. (2000). Emerging judicial strategies for the mentally ill in the criminal caseload: Mental health courts in Fort Lauderdale, Seattle, San Bernadino, & Anchorage. *Bureau of Justice Assistance*. Retrieved from www.ncjs.gov/pdffiles1/bja/182304.pdf.

Goldstein, H. (1990). *Problem-oriented policing*. New York: McGraw-Hill.

Gondolf, E. (1999). A comparison of four batterer intervention systems. *Journal of Interpersonal Violence, 14*(1), 41–61.

Griffin, P. A., Steadman, H. J., & Petrila, J. (2002). The use of criminal charges and sanctions in Mental Health Courts. *Psychiatric Services, 53*(10), 1285–1289.

Grudzinskas, A. J., Clayfield, J. C., Roy-Bujnowski, K., Fisher, W. H., & Richardson, M. H. (2005). Integrating the criminal justice system into mental health service delivery: The Worchester Diversion experience. *Behavioral Sciences and the Law, 23*, 277–293.

Hails, J., & Borum, R. (2003). Police training and specialized approaches to respond to people with mental illnesses. *Crime & Delinquency, 49*, 52–61.

Haimowitz, S. (2002). Can Mental Health Courts end the criminalization of persons with mental illness? *Psychiatric Services, 53*(10), 1226–1228.

Harrell, A., & Bryer, S. (1998). The process evaluation of project connection lessons on linking Drug Courts and communities. *The Urban Institute*.

Harrell, A., & Roman, J. (2001). Reducing drug use and crime among offenders: The impact of graduated sanctions. *Journal of Drug Issues, 31*(1), 207–231.

Hart, B., & Klein, A. F. (2013). *Practical implication of current IPV research for victim advocates and service providers*. Washington, D.C. NIJ OJP NCJR 244388.

Hasselbrack, A. M. (2001). Opting in to Mental Health Courts. *Corrections Compendium, 26*(10), 4.

Henning, K., Jones, A., & Holdford, R. (2003). Treatment need of women arrested for domestic violence. *Journal of Interpersonal Violence, 87*(8), 839–856.

Henrinck, H. A., Swart, S. C., Ama, S. M., Dolezal, C. D., & King, S. (2005). Rearrest and linkage to mental health services among clients of Clark County Mental Health Court program. *Psychiatric Services, 56*(7), 853–857.

Hoge,S., Bonnie, R., Poythress, N., & Monahan, J. (1999) *The MacArthur competence assessment tool criminal adjudication*. Psychological Assessment Resources.

Hser, Y., Teryuna, C., Brown, A.H., Huang, D., et al. (2007). Impact of California's Proposition 36 on the drug system: Treatment capacity and displacement. *American Journal of Public Health, 97*(1). *Jackson v. Indiana (406 U.S. 715, 1972)*.

Jungersen, T., Walker, L. E. A., Black, R., & Groth, C. (in press). Trauma treatment for intimate partner violence in incarcerated populations. *Journal of Counseling Development*.

Kelling, G. L. (1988). *Police and communities: The quiet revolution*. Washington, D.C.: National Institute of Justice.

Kondo, L. L. (2001). Advocacy of the establishment of Mental Health Specialty Courts in the provisions of therapeutic justice for mentally ill offenders. *American Journal of Criminal Law, 28*(3), 255–366.

Kleinman, T. G., & Walker, L. E. A. (2014). Protecting psychotherapy clients from the shadow of the law: A call for the revision of the Association of Family and Conciliation Court (AFCC) Guidelines for court-involved therapy. *Journal of Child Custody, 11*, 335–362.

Krakowski, M. (2005). Schizophrenia with aggressive and violent behaviors. *Psychiatric Annals, 35*(1), 44–49.

Kupers, T. A. (2001). Psychotherapy with men in prisons. In G. R. Brooks & G. E. Good (Eds.), *The New handbook of psychotherapy and counseling with men: A comprehensive guide to settings, problems, and treatment approaches* (pp. 172–185). San Francisco, CA: Jossey-Bass Inc.

Lamb, R. H., & Weinberger, L. E. (2008). Mental Health Courts as a way to provide treatment to violent persons with severe mental illness. *Journal of the American Medical Association, 300* (6), 722–724.

Lamb, R. H., Weinberger, L. E., & DeCuir, W. J. (2002). The police and mental health. *Psychiatric Services, 53*(10), 1266–1271.

Lamberti, J. S., Weisman, R. L., Schwarzkopf, S. B., Price, N., Ashton, R. M., & Trompeter, J. (2001). The mentally ill in jails and prisons: Toward an integrated model of prevention. *Psychiatric Quaterly, 72*(1), 63–77.

Lamberti, J. S., & Weisman, R. L. (2004). Persons with severe mental disorders in the criminal justice system: Challenges and opportunities. *Psychiatric Quarterly, 75*, 151–164.

Lerner-Wren, G. (2000). Broward's mental health court: An innovative approach to the mentally disabled in the criminal justice system. *The National Center for State Courts.* Retrieved from http://ojp.usdoj.gov/bja/evaluationpsi_courts/mh6.htm.

Lerner-Wren, G., & Appel, A. R. (2001). A court for the nonviolent defendant with a mental disability. *Psychiatric Annals, 31*(7), 453–458.

Lewis, C. (2006). Treating incarcerated women: Gender matters. *Psychiatric Clinics of North America, 7*(1), 773–789.

Link, B. G., Monahan, J., Stueve, A., & Cullen, F. T. (1999). Real in their consequences: A sociological approach to understanding the association between psychotic symptoms and violence. *American Sociological Review, 64*, 316–332.

Linquist, C. H., Krebs, C. P., & Lattimore, P. K. (2006). Sanctions and rewards in Drug Court programs: Implementation, perceived efficacy, and decision making. *Journal of Drug Issues, 36*(1).

Lopez, V. A., Mahler, C. Lundell, L., Guzkowski, K., Walker, L. E. A., & Van Hasselt, V. B. (2014, August). The victimization of women through murder-suicide: Florida case examples. Poster presented at the American Psychological Annual Convention, Washington, D.C.

Lovell, D., & Jemelka, R. (1998). Coping with mental illness in prisons. *Family and Community Health, 21*(3), 54–66.

Lowenkamp, C., Holsinger, A., & Latessa, E. (2005). Are drug courts effective? A meta analytic review. *Journal of Community Corrections, Fall,* 5–28.

Lurigio, A. J., Rollins, A., & Fallon, J. (2004). The effects of serious mental illness on offender reentry. *Federal Probation, 68*(2), 45–52.

Maier, G. J., & Fulton, L. (1998). Inpatient treatment of offenders with mental illness. In R. M. Weinstein (Ed.), *Treatment of offenders with mental disorders* (pp. 211–264). New York, NY: The Guilford Press.

Malcolm, A. S., Van Hasselt, V. B., & Russell, S. (in press). Police response to the mentally ill: An evaluative review. *Victims and Offenders.*

Tucker, A. S., Van Hasselt, V. B., & Russell, S. (2008). Law enforcement response to the mentally ill: An evaluative review. *Brief Treatment and Crisis Intervention, 8*, 236–250.

Marans, S. (1996). Psychoanalysis on the beat: Children, police and urban trauma. In Solnit, A., Neubauer, P., Abrams, & Dowling, A. S. The psychoanalytic study of the child, 522–541. New Haven, Connecticut: Yale University Press.

Marans, S., Berkowitz, S., & Cohen, D. (1998). Police and mental health professionals. Collaborative responses to the impact of violence on children and families. *Child and Adolescent Psychiatric Clinics of North America, 7*(3), 635–651.

Mastrowski, S. D. (1988). Community policing as reform: A cautionary tale. In J. R. Greene & S. D. Mastrowski (Eds.), *Community policing: Rhetoric or reality.* New York: Praeger.

Mastrowski, S. D., Worden, R. E., & Snipes, J. B. (1995). Law enforcement in a time of community policing. *Criminology, 33,* 539–563.

McCampbell, S. W. (2001). Mental Health Courts: What sheriffs need to know. *Sheriff, 53*(2), 40–43.

McNiel, D. E., Binder, R. L., & Robinson, J. C. (2005). Incarceration associated with homelessness, mental disorder, and co-occurring substance abuse. *Psychiatric Services, 56*(7), 840.

Miller, J. M., & Shutt, J. E. (2001). Considering the need for empirically grounded Drug Court screening mechanisms. *Journal of Drug Issues, 31*(1), 91–106.

Miller, Susan. (2001). The paradox of women arrested for domestic violence. *Violence Against Women, 7*(12), 1339–1376.

Moore, M. (1994). Research synthesis and police implications. In D. Rosenbaum (Ed.), *The challenge of community policing: Testing the promises* (pp. 285–299). Thousand Oaks, CA: Sage.

Munetz, M. R., & Griffin, R. A. (2006). Use of the Sequential Intercept Model as an approach to decriminalization of people with serious mental illness. *Psychiatric Services, 57*(4), 544–549.

National GAINS Center for People with Co-Occurring Disorders in the Justice System. (1999). *Blending funds to pay for criminal justice diversion for people with co-occurring disorders.* Fact Sheet Series- Delmar, NY: The National GAINS Center for People with Co-Occurring Disorders in the Justice System.

National GAINS Center for People with Co-Occurring Disorders in the Justice System. (2001). *The prevalence of co-occurring Mental illness and substance use disorders in jails. Fact sheet series.* Delmar, NY: The National GAINS Center.

National GAINS Center for People with Co-Occurring Disorders in the Justice System. (2002). *The Nathaniel project: An alternative to incarceration program for people with serious mental illness who have committed felony offenses.* Program Brief Series. Delmar, NY: The National GAINS Center.

National Institute of Justice. (2006). *Drug Courts: The second decade.* http://www.ojp.usdoj.gov/nij/pubs-sum/211081.htm.

National Mental Health Association. (2003). *Jail diversion for people with mental illness: Developing supportive community coalitions.* Delmar, NY: The TAPA Center for Jail Diversion.

O'Keefe, K. (2006). *The Brooklyn Mental Health Court evaluation: Planning, implementation, courtroom dynamics, and participant outcomes.* New York, NY: Center for Court Innovation.

O'Keefe, K. (2007). The Brooklyn Mental Health Court: Implementation and outcomes. In G. Berman & M. Rempel (Eds.), *Documenting results: Research on problem-solving justice* (pp. 281–318). New York: Center for Court Innovation.

Poythress, N. G., Petrila, J., McGaha, A., & Boothroyd, R. (2002). Perceived coercion and procedural justice in the Broward mental health court. *International Journal of Law and Psychiatry, 25,* 517–533.

President's New Freedom Commission on Mental Health (2003, July). *Final report to the President: Executive summary.* Retrieved June 6, 2008, from http://www.mentalhealthcommission.gov/subcommittee/sub_chairs.htm.

Redlich, A. D. (2005). Voluntary, but knowing and intelligent? Comprehension in mental health courts. *Psychology: Public Policy and the Law, 11,* 605–619.

Redlich, A. D., Steadman, H. J., Monahan, J., Petrila, J., & Griffin, P. (2006). The second generation of Mental Health Courts. *Psychology, Public, Policy, and the Law.*

Reiss, A. J. (1985). *Policing a city's central district: The Oakland story.* Washington, DC: National Institute of Justice.

Reuland, M., & Margolis, G. (2003). Police approaches that improve the response to people with mental illnesses: A focus on victims. *The Police Chief, 11*, 35–39.

Rice, M. E., & Harris, G. T. (1997). The treatment of mentally disordered offenders. *Psychology, Public Policy, and Law, 3*(1), 126–183.

Roesch, R., Zapf, P., & Eaves, D. (2006). *Fitness interview test-revised.* Professional Resource Press.

Rosenbaum, D. P. (1988). Community crime prevention: A review and synthesis of the literature. *Justice Quarterly, 5*, 323–395.

Roskes, E., & Feldman, R. (1999). A collaborative community-based treatment program for offenders with mental illness. *Psychiatric Services, 50*, 1614–1619.

Ruddell, R., Roy, B., & Diehl, S. (2004). Diverting offenders with mental illness from jail- A tale of two states. *Corrections Compendium, 29*(5).

Ruddell, R. (2006). Jail interventions for inmates with mental illnesses. *Journal of Correctional Health Care, 12*(2), 118–131.

Saum, C. A., Scarpitti, S. F., & Robbins, C. A. (2001). Violent offenders in Drug Court. *Journal of Drug Issues, 31*(1), 107–128.

Saunders, D. G., Faller, K. C., & Tolman, R. M. (2010). Child custody evaluator's beliefs about domestic abuse allegations: Their relationship to evaluator demographics, background, domestic violence knowledge, and custody visitation recommendations. U.S. DOJ, NIJ, OLP, WG-Bx-0013.

Sechrest,D.K., & Shicor, D. (2001). Determinants of graduation from a day treatment Drug Court in California: A preliminary study. *Journal of Drug Issues, 31*(1).

Shepard, M., & Rashchick, M. (1999). How child welfare workers assess and intervene around issues of domestic violence. *Child Maltreatment, 4*(2), 148–156.

Sheridan, E. P., & Teplin, L. (1981). Police-referred psychiatric emergencies: Advantages of community treatment. *Journal of Community Psychology, 9*, 140–147.

Silberberg, J. M., Vital, T. L., & Brakel, S. J. (2001). Breaking down barriers to mandated outpatient treatment for mentally ill offenders. *Psychiatric Annals, 31*(7), 433.

Skeem, J. L., & Eno-Louden, J. (2006). Toward evidence-based practice for probationers and parolees mandated to mental health treatment. *Psychiatric Services, 57*(3), 333–341.

Skolnick, J. H., & Bailey, D. H. (1986). *The new blue line: Police innovations in six American cities.* New York: Free Press.

Slate, R. N., Feldman, R., Roskes, E., & Baerga, M. (2004). Training federal probation officers as mental health specialists. *Federal Probation, 68*(3), 9–15.

Slate, R. N., Roskes, E., Feldman, R., & Baerga, M. (2003). Doing justice for mental illness and society: Federal probation and pretrial services officers as mental health specialists. *Federal Probation, 67*(3), 13–19.

Spohn, C., Piper, R. K., Martin, T., & Frenzel, E. D. (2001). Drug Courts and recidivism: The results of an evaluation using two comparison groups and multiple indicators of recidivism. *Journal of Drug Issues, 31*(1), 149–176.

Stafford, K. P., & Wygant, D. B. (2005). The role of competency to stand trial in mental health courts. *Behavioral Sciences and the Law, 23*, 245–258.

Steadman, H. J. (n.d.). *Jail diversion: Creating alternatives for persons with mental illnesses.* Delmar, NY: National GAINS Center for People with Co-Occurring Disorders in the Justice System. [Brochure].

Steadman, H., Deane, M., Borum, R., & Morrissey, J. (2000). Comparing outcomes of major models of police responses to mental health emergencies. *Psychiatric Services, 51*, 645–649.

Steadman, H. J., & Naples, M. (2005). Assessing the effectiveness of jail diversion programs for persons with serious mental illness and co-occurring substance disorders. *Behavioral Sciences and the Law, 23*, 163–170.

Steadman, H. J., Redlich, A. D., Griffin, P., Petrila, J., & Monahan, J. (2005). From referral to disposition: Case processing in seven Mental Health Courts. *Behavioral Sciences and the Law, 23*, 215–226.

Strauss, G., Glenn, P., Reddi, P., Afaq, I., Podolskaya, A., Rybakova, T., et al. (2005). Psychiatric disposition of patients brought in by crisis intervention-team police officers. *Community Mental Health Journal, 41*, 223–228.

Supreme Court of Florida. (2007). *Mental health: transforming Florida's mental health system. Constructing a comprehensive and competent criminal justice/mental health/substance abuse treatment system: Strategies for planning, leadership, financing, and service development.* Retrieved from www.nicic.org/library/022708.

Sykes, G. (1986). Street justice: A moral defense of order maintenance. *Justice Quarterly, 3*, 497–512.

Tang, J. J. (2010). An examination of competency restoration in a South Florida community-based setting. Dissertation submitted to Nova Southeastern University.

Teller, J. L. S., Muntetz, M. R., Gil, K. M., & Ritter, C. (2006). Crisis intervention team training for police officers responding to mental disturbance calls. *Psychiatric Services, 57*, 232–237.

Teplin, L. A. (1983). The criminalization of the mentally ill: Speculation in search of data. *Psychological Bulletin, 94*, 54–67.

Teplin, L. A. (1984). Criminalizing mental disorder: The comparative arrest rates of the mentally ill. *American Psychologist, 39*, 794–803.

Teplin, L. A., & Pruett, N. S. (1992). Police as street-corner psychiatrist: Managing the mentally ill. *International Journal of Law and Psychiatry, 15*, 139–156.

Turley, A., Thornton, T., Johnson, C., & Azzolino, S. (2004). Jail drug and alcohol treatment program reduces recidivism in nonviolent offenders: A longitudinal study of Monroe County, New York's, Jail treatment drug and alcohol program. *International Journal of Offender Therapy and Comparative Criminology, 48*(6), 721–728.

Tyuse, S. W., & Linhorst, D. M. (2005). Drug Courts and Mental Health Courts: Implications for social work. *Health and Social Work, 30*(3), 233–240.

U.S. Department of Justice. (2005). *Office of justice programs; Bureau of Justice Statistics; family violence statistics including statistics on strangers and acquaintances.* Retrieved November 6, 2006, from http://www.ojp.usdoj.gov/bjs/abstract/fvs.htm.

U.S. Department of Justice. (2006). *Mental health problems of prison and jail inmates.* Prepared by D.J. James & L.E. Glaze. Retrieved June 23, 2007, from http://www.ojp.usdoj.gov/bjs/pub/pdf/mhppji.pdf.

U.S. vs Dusky.

Vickers, B. (2000). *Memphis, Tennessee, police department's crisis intervention team.* Bulletin From the Field, Practitioner Perspectives: U.S. Department of Justice.

Walker, L. E. A. (2009). *Battered Woman Syndrome* (3rd ed.). New York: Springer.

Walker, L. E. A., Cummings, D. M., & Cummings, N. A. (Eds.). (2012). *Our broken Family Court System.* New York: Ithaca Press.

Walker, L. E. A., Waxman, C., McKown, K., Jaslow, M., Gaviria, G., Glick, R., et al. (2012). *Efficacy of the Felony Mental Health Court.* Unpublished Report submitted to the Chief Judge of Broward Felony Mental Health Court.

Watson, A., Hanrahan, P., Luchins, D., & Lurigio, A. (2001). Mental Health Courts and the complex issues of mentally ill offenders. *Psychiatric Services, 52*, 477–481.

Weisel, D., & Eck, J. (1994). Toward a practical approach to organizational change: community policing initiative in six cities. In D. Rosenbaum (Ed.), *The Challenge of community policing: Testing the promises.* Thousand Oaks, CA: Sage.

Wexler, D. B. (2008). Two decades of the therapeutic jurisprudence. *Touro Law Review, 24*, 17–29.

Winick, B. J. (1999). Redefining the role of the criminal defense lawyer at plea bargaining and sentencing: Therapeutic jurisprudence/preventive law model. *Psychology, Public Policy & the Law, 5,* 1034–1083.

Wolf, E., & Colyer, C. (2001). Everyday hassles: Barriers to recovery in Drug Court. *Journal of Drug Issues, 31*(1), 233–258.

Wolfe, E. L., Guydish, J., Woods, W., & Tajima, B. (2004). Perspectives on the Drug Court model across systems: A process evaluation. *Journal of Psychoactive Drugs, 36*(3).

Wolfer, L. (2006). Graduates speak: A qualitative exploration of Drug Court graduates' views of the strengths and weaknesses of the program. *Contemporary Drug Problems, 33*(2).

Made in the USA
Middletown, DE
07 January 2017